LATIN AMERICAN POLITICAL, ECONOMIC, AND SECURITY ISSUES

EL SALVADOR

CONDITIONS, ISSUES AND U.S. RELATIONS

LATIN AMERICAN POLITICAL, ECONOMIC, AND SECURITY ISSUES

Additional books in this series can be found on Nova's website under the Series tab.

Additional e-books in this series can be found on Nova's website under the e-book tab.

LATIN AMERICAN POLITICAL, ECONOMIC, AND SECURITY ISSUES

EL SALVADOR

CONDITIONS, ISSUES AND U.S. RELATIONS

JOELLE FOSTER
EDITOR

Copyright © 2014 by Nova Science Publishers, Inc.

All rights reserved. No part of this book may be reproduced, stored in a retrieval system or transmitted in any form or by any means: electronic, electrostatic, magnetic, tape, mechanical photocopying, recording or otherwise without the written permission of the Publisher.

For permission to use material from this book please contact us:
Telephone 631-231-7269; Fax 631-231-8175
Web Site: http://www.novapublishers.com

NOTICE TO THE READER

The Publisher has taken reasonable care in the preparation of this book, but makes no expressed or implied warranty of any kind and assumes no responsibility for any errors or omissions. No liability is assumed for incidental or consequential damages in connection with or arising out of information contained in this book. The Publisher shall not be liable for any special, consequential, or exemplary damages resulting, in whole or in part, from the readers' use of, or reliance upon, this material. Any parts of this book based on government reports are so indicated and copyright is claimed for those parts to the extent applicable to compilations of such works.

Independent verification should be sought for any data, advice or recommendations contained in this book. In addition, no responsibility is assumed by the publisher for any injury and/or damage to persons or property arising from any methods, products, instructions, ideas or otherwise contained in this publication.

This publication is designed to provide accurate and authoritative information with regard to the subject matter covered herein. It is sold with the clear understanding that the Publisher is not engaged in rendering legal or any other professional services. If legal or any other expert assistance is required, the services of a competent person should be sought. FROM A DECLARATION OF PARTICIPANTS JOINTLY ADOPTED BY A COMMITTEE OF THE AMERICAN BAR ASSOCIATION AND A COMMITTEE OF PUBLISHERS.

Additional color graphics may be available in the e-book version of this book.

Library of Congress Cataloging-in-Publication Data

ISBN: 978-1-63321-766-9

Published by Nova Science Publishers, Inc. † New York

CONTENTS

Preface vii

Chapter 1 El Salvador: Background and U.S. Relations 1
Clare Ribando Seelke

Chapter 2 Partnership for Growth El Salvador-United States,
Six Month Scorecard: November 2013-May 2014 35
U.S. Department of State

Chapter 3 El Salvador 2013 Human Rights Report 51
*U.S. Department of State; Bureau of Democracy,
Human Rights and Labor*

Chapter 4 El Salvador 2012 International Religious
Freedom Report 81
*U.S. Department of State;
Bureau of Democracy, Human Rights and Labor*

Chapter 5 2014 Investment Climate Statement: El Salvador 85
Bureau of Economic and Business Affairs

Index 111

PREFACE

This book discusses the issues and the U.S. relations with El Salvador. It also examines its current conditions.

Chapter 1 – Congress has maintained interest in El Salvador, a small Central American country that has a large percentage of its population living in the United States, since the country's civil conflict (1980-1992). Whereas in the 1980s the U.S. government spent billions of dollars supporting the Salvadoran government's efforts against the Farabundo Marti National Liberation Front (FMLN) insurgency, the United States is now working with the country's second consecutive democratically-elected FMLN Administration. Despite the potential challenges involved for both sides, analysts predict that U.S.-Salvadoran relations will remain constructive during Salvador Sánchez Cerén's presidency, as they did during Mauricio Funes' term (2009-2014). El Salvador is facing significant economic and security challenges that the country is unlikely to be able to address without substantial external support. El Salvador posted an economic growth rate of just 1.4% in 2013, the lowest of any country in Central America. The government is running high deficits and attracting little foreign investment. Economists have cited security concerns as a barrier to investment. Although a truce between the country's gangs helped lower homicide rates in 2012 and 2013, it has unraveled and violent crime is increasing. Inaugurated to a five-year term on June 1, 2014, President Salvador Sánchez Cerén, a former FMLN guerrilla commander, took office pledging to lead a government based on the principles of "honor, austerity, efficiency and transparency." After defeating the conservative Nationalist Republican Alliance (ARENA) candidate, Norman Quijano, by just over 6,000 votes in a runoff election held in March, President Sánchez Cerén has adopted a conciliatory attitude. Cooperation with the opposition and the private sector will likely be necessary in order for President

Sánchez Cerén to address the serious challenges he inherited. Since the FMLN lacks a majority in the National Assembly, it will have to form coalitions in order to pass legislation. This could change, however, after the March 2015 legislative elections. The direction that bilateral relations take will likely depend upon the degree to which the Sánchez Cerén government maintains security and economic cooperation with the United States under the Partnership for Growth (PFG) initiative. El Salvador is the only Latin American country that has been selected to participate in the PFG, an initiative launched in 2011 that commits both governments to work closely together in a variety of areas. Congress has provided bilateral assistance, which totaled an estimated $22.3 million in FY2014, as well as regional security assistance provided through the Central American Regional Security Initiative (CARSI) to support PFG priorities, including anti-gang and antidrug efforts. Cooperation in boosting El Salvador's competitiveness could be bolstered by a second $277 million Millennium Challenge Corporation (MCC) compact. The MCC Board has approved the agreement, but it has yet to be signed. Should President Sánchez Cerén orient his policies too much toward Venezuela or fail to combat corruption, there could be congressional opposition to funding that second compact. In addition to security and economic cooperation, migration issues, such has how to prevent emigration by unaccompanied children from El Salvador and how to reintegrate deportees from the United States into Salvadoran society, are likely to figure prominently on the bilateral agenda. This report examines current conditions in El Salvador as well as issues in U.S.-Salvadoran relations.

Chapter 2 – Report of Partnership for Growth El Salvador-United States, Six Month Scorecard: November 2013-May 2014.

Chapter 3 – El Salvador is a constitutional multi-party republic. In 2009 voters elected Carlos Mauricio Funes Cartagena of the Farabundo Marti National Liberation Front (FMLN) as president for a five-year term in generally free and fair elections. Free and fair legislative assembly and municipal elections took place in March 2012. Authorities failed at times to maintain effective control over the security forces. Security forces committed human rights abuses. The principal human rights problems were widespread corruption; weaknesses in the judiciary and the security forces that contributed to a high level of impunity; and abuse, including domestic violence, discrimination, and commercial sexual exploitation against women and children. Other human rights problems included isolated unlawful killings and cruel treatment by security forces; lengthy pretrial detention; harsh and life-threatening prison conditions; some restrictions on freedom of speech and press; trafficking in persons; and discrimination against persons with disabilities and persons with HIV/AIDS. There was also widespread discrimination and some violence against lesbian, gay, bisexual, and transgender (LGBT) persons. Child labor and inadequate enforcement of labor laws also were problems. Impunity persisted despite the government taking steps to dismiss some officials who committed abuses in the penitentiary system and within the police force.

Chapter 4 – The constitution and other laws and policies protect religious freedom and, in practice, the government generally respected religious freedom. The trend in the government's respect for religious freedom did not change significantly during the year. There were no reports of societal abuses or discrimination based on religious affiliation, belief, or practice. U.S. embassy officials met periodically with government officials, religious leaders, and university officials to discuss religious freedom.

Chapter 5 – El Salvador is eager to attract greater foreign investment and is taking steps to improve its investment climate. In recent years, El Salvador has lagged the region in terms of attraction of Foreign Direct Investment (FDI). The Central Bank of El Salvador reported that FDI reached just $140.0 million in 2013, a 71 percent decline from the $481.9 million received in 2012. Political uncertainty, burdensome commercial regulations, a sometimes ineffective judicial system, and widespread violent crime are often cited as elements that impede investment in El Salvador. In 2011, El Salvador and the United States initiated the Partnership for Growth (PFG), a new cooperative development model, to help improve El Salvador's economy and investment climate. November 2013 marked the second anniversary of PFG implementation, and the partnership has taken steps to foster a more favorable environment for business and investment, and improve human capital and infrastructure. For more information on PFG, please access the link on the Embassy's website at http://sansalvador. usembassy.gov/. CAFTA-DR, the free trade agreement among Central American countries, the Dominican Republic, and the United States, entered into force for the United States and El Salvador in 2006. El Salvador also has free trade agreements with Mexico, Chile, Panama, Colombia, and Taiwan. All have entered into force with the exception of the FTA with Colombia which is expected to be activated soon. El Salvador, jointly with Costa Rica, Guatemala, Honduras, Nicaragua, and Panama, signed an Association Agreement with the European Union that includes the establishment of a Free Trade Area. El Salvador is also negotiating trade agreements with Canada, Peru, and Belize. In October 2012, the Salvadoran government presented to the Legislative Assembly a package of legislation to promote investment and facilitate commerce. Some of these laws have been passed including reforms to the International Services Law and Free Trade Zone Law, and the Construction Simplification Law. In April 2014, the Legislative Assembly approved reforms to address shortcomings in a Public-Private Partnership (PPP) Law that was originally passed in May 2013. The law and associated reforms were designed to provide a legal framework for the development of PPP projects and create a more suitable environment for investment.

In: El Salvador
Editor: Joelle Foster

ISBN: 978-1-63321-766-9
© 2014 Nova Science Publishers, Inc.

Chapter 1

EL SALVADOR: BACKGROUND AND U.S. RELATIONS[*]

Clare Ribando Seelke

SUMMARY

Congress has maintained interest in El Salvador, a small Central American country that has a large percentage of its population living in the United States, since the country's civil conflict (1980-1992). Whereas in the 1980s the U.S. government spent billions of dollars supporting the Salvadoran government's efforts against the Farabundo Marti National Liberation Front (FMLN) insurgency, the United States is now working with the country's second consecutive democratically-elected FMLN Administration. Despite the potential challenges involved for both sides, analysts predict that U.S.-Salvadoran relations will remain constructive during Salvador Sánchez Cerén's presidency, as they did during Mauricio Funes' term (2009-2014).

El Salvador is facing significant economic and security challenges that the country is unlikely to be able to address without substantial external support. El Salvador posted an economic growth rate of just 1.4% in 2013, the lowest of any country in Central America. The government is running high deficits and attracting little foreign investment. Economists have cited security concerns as a barrier to investment. Although a truce

---

[*] This is an edited, reformatted and augmented version of a Congressional Research Service publication, No. R43616, dated June 23, 2014.

between the country's gangs helped lower homicide rates in 2012 and 2013, it has unraveled and violent crime is increasing.

Inaugurated to a five-year term on June 1, 2014, President Salvador Sánchez Cerén, a former FMLN guerrilla commander, took office pledging to lead a government based on the principles of "honor, austerity, efficiency and transparency." After defeating the conservative Nationalist Republican Alliance (ARENA) candidate, Norman Quijano, by just over 6,000 votes in a runoff election held in March, President Sánchez Cerén has adopted a conciliatory attitude. Cooperation with the opposition and the private sector will likely be necessary in order for President Sánchez Cerén to address the serious challenges he inherited. Since the FMLN lacks a majority in the National Assembly, it will have to form coalitions in order to pass legislation. This could change, however, after the March 2015 legislative elections.

The direction that bilateral relations take will likely depend upon the degree to which the Sánchez Cerén government maintains security and economic cooperation with the United States under the Partnership for Growth (PFG) initiative. El Salvador is the only Latin American country that has been selected to participate in the PFG, an initiative launched in 2011 that commits both governments to work closely together in a variety of areas. Congress has provided bilateral assistance, which totaled an estimated $22.3 million in FY2014, as well as regional security assistance provided through the Central American Regional Security Initiative (CARSI) to support PFG priorities, including anti-gang and antidrug efforts. Cooperation in boosting El Salvador's competitiveness could be bolstered by a second $277 million Millennium Challenge Corporation (MCC) compact. The MCC Board has approved the agreement, but it has yet to be signed. Should President Sánchez Cerén orient his policies too much toward Venezuela or fail to combat corruption, there could be congressional opposition to funding that second compact.

In addition to security and economic cooperation, migration issues, such has how to prevent emigration by unaccompanied children from El Salvador and how to reintegrate deportees from the United States into Salvadoran society, are likely to figure prominently on the bilateral agenda.

This report examines current conditions in El Salvador as well as issues in U.S.-Salvadoran relations.

INTRODUCTION

A small, densely-populated Central American country that has deep historical, familial, and economic ties to the United States; El Salvador has long been a focus of congressional interest (see **Figure 1** for a map and key data on the country).[1] After a troubled history of authoritarian rule and a brutal civil war (1980-1992), El Salvador has made strides over the past two decades in establishing a multiparty democracy. A peace accord negotiated in 1992 brought the war to an end and assimilated the leftist Farabundo Marti National Liberation Front (FMLN) guerrilla movement into the political process as a political party. In 2009, Mauricio Funes, a former journalist, took office as head of the country's first FMLN government.[2] After a razor-thin election, Salvador Sánchez Cerén, the last living FMLN high commander, took office on June 1, 2014, at the helm of a government composed mainly of former guerrillas. The new government's success could hinge on its ability to work with conservative parties, the private sector, and foreign partners (including the United States) to overcome the country's challenges.

After the peace accords were signed, successive rightist Nationalist Republican Alliance (ARENA) governments in the 1990s-2000s sought to rebuild democracy and implement market-friendly economic reforms. ARENA proved to be a reliable U.S. ally and presided over a period of economic growth, but was unable to effectively address some of the country's deep-seeded problems, including inequality, violence, and corruption. Former ARENA president Francisco Flores (1999-2004) reportedly fled to Panama in 2014 after being charged with embezzling and mishandling some $15 million in donations from Taiwan that were meant for earthquake relief.[3] The Salvadoran government is seeking his extradition. Allegations of corruption have dogged former president Anthony ("Tony") Saca (2004-2009) as well.[4] Under ARENA governments, socioeconomic development advanced, but was hindered by natural disasters, including earthquakes in 2001 and several hurricanes.

Deep scars remain evident today from a war that resulted in significant human rights violations, more than 70,000 deaths, and massive emigration to the United States.[5] Old wounds could be reopened should the Salvadoran Supreme Court overturn the 1993 Amnesty Law that has shielded those who committed human rights abuses during the civil conflict from prosecution. Still, many argue that such a decision could provide justice for victims and advance human rights in the country. Some analysts maintain that the history of U.S. involvement in countering the insurgency in El Salvador could make relations between the United States and this current FMLN government difficult for both sides.[6]

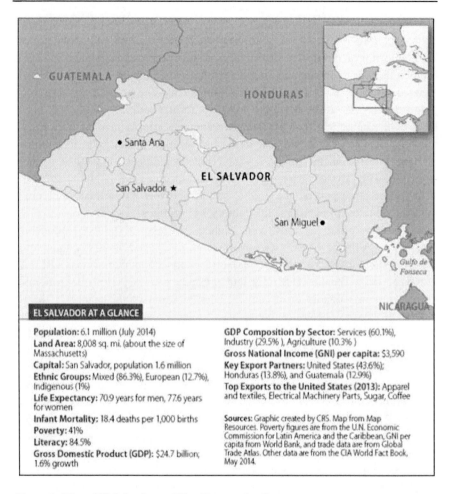

Figure 1. Map of El Salvador and Key Data on the Country.

POLITICAL CONDITIONS

Funes Government (2009-2014)

Mauricio Funes, a former journalist elected in March 2009 to lead the country's first FMLN government, remained popular throughout his term, but his Administration struggled to address many of the country's deeply entrenched economic and security problems. Funes was an independent who had periodic conflicts with members of the FMLN, including his Vice President, Salvador Sánchez Cerén. In order to secure passage of legislation, President Funes had to form coalitions with other parties, namely the populist Grand Alliance for National Unity (GANA) party formed by former President Tony Saca after he split from ARENA in 2009.

Funes has been credited with developing a variety of social programs. One of the more popular programs his government established provided uniforms, school supplies, and lunches to public school students. Another, designed and overseen by then-First Lady and Minister of Social Inclusion Vanda Pignato, involved the creation of five multifaceted women's health centers throughout the country under a program known as *Ciudad Mujer*. Perhaps as a result of those efforts, some 65.9% of Salvadorans polled in May 2014 rated Funes' Administration positively even while acknowledging that security and economic conditions had worsened during his term. [7]

In the area of human rights, President Funes issued a historic apology to victims of the 1981 El Mozote massacre on the 20th anniversary of the signing of the Peace Accords. He "recognized" the Inter American Court of Human Rights ruling that El Salvador needs to reinvestigate the massacre and guarantee the rights of victims to seek reparations. He did not push for a repeal of the country's amnesty law nor urge the Salvadoran Supreme Court to extradite military officers to Spain to stand trial for their roles in the 1989 murders of Jesuit priests.[8]

While the Salvadoran public may evaluate the Funes government favorably, it has been criticized by analysts from both the right and left for failing to bolster economic growth (see "Economic and Social Conditions") below, reduce crime, or fight corruption. The Funes government expanded crime prevention programs and community policing efforts, but its security policy will likely be remembered for the way it tacitly supported and then later disavowed a truce between the country's largest gangs. Observers have criticized Funes' inability to improve transparency and accountability, particularly in the military and police.[9]

The Funes Administration was also fraught with disputes among the Supreme Court, National Assembly, and executive branch over the separation of powers and clashes between the government and the Salvadoran private sector. Although President Funes criticized some of the court's decisions and initially challenged its authority, he did abide by its rulings, including a decision rendering his prior appointments of retired generals to lead the Ministry of Public Security and Justice and Civilian National Police (PNC), which falls under that ministry, unconstitutional. From June to August 2012, the country became embroiled in a constitutional crisis over the make-up and authority of El Salvador's Supreme Court that was only settled after a series of complicated negotiations led by President Funes himself. Nevertheless, some critics have decried Funes for causing conflict with the private sector and improperly wielding his power on behalf of the FMLN.[10]

2014 Elections: Results and Implications[11]

On February 2, 2014, El Salvador held the first round of its 2014 presidential elections. Despite a polarized electoral climate, election day proved to be relatively peaceful, albeit with low turnout of 50% (compared to 65% in the 2009 elections). Vice President Salvador Sánchez Cerén came close to winning in the first round, with 49% of the vote, 10% more than the ARENA's candidate, Norman Quijano, a two-term mayor of San Salvador. Former president Tony Saca who headed a center-right "UNIDAD" or "Unity Movement" coalition led by the GANA party he started in 2009 likely siphoned voters from Quijano by garnering 11.4% of the vote. Because no candidate won the required 50% of the votes cast, a runoff election had to be held.

The March 9, 2014 runoff election between Sánchez Cerén and Quijano proved to be much closer than expected. During the run-up to the second round of voting, ARENA worked to capture Saca voters and encourage new voters to head to the polls. ARENA promised to continue the popular social programs started under Funes, but also took advantage of media reports of protests occurring in Venezuela to warn voters of what could happen under a radical FMLN government.

El Salvador's Electoral Tribunal did not certify the final results until it and the Supreme Court had dismissed all but one of ARENA's challenges to the validity of the results on March 25, 2014. The final results showed Sánchez Cerén capturing 50.1% of the vote and Quijano receiving 49.9%. Secretary of State John Kerry congratulated Sánchez Cerén on his victory in a statement following the certification.[12] ARENA accepted the results the following day and promised to be a loyal opposition party. Sánchez Cerén's extremely narrow margin of victory revealed the country's ongoing polarization between left and right. Prior to taking office, President-elect Sánchez Cerén and Vice President Oscar Ortiz adopted a conciliatory approach toward ARENA and the private sector, convening public and private dialogues between the transition team and different sectors of Salvadoran society.

Sánchez Cerén Administration

Composition and Priorities

During the presidential campaign, Salvador Sánchez Cerén sought to broaden his appeal beyond FMLN militants by running as a "progressive" and not as a hardliner. He selected Oscar Ortiz, the popular mayor of Santa Tecla, as his Vice President and ran on a "Deepen the Change" platform. Sánchez Cerén promised to keep the social programs that have been popular during the Funes government, but did not discuss controversial policies, such as the gang truce. President Sánchez Cerén's Cabinet includes several holdovers from the Funes government, including the Ministers of the Economy, Foreign Affairs, Public Works, and Social Inclusion. Several of those ministers have formed good working relationships with U.S. officials and have participated in the PFG and MCC compact process. The Cabinet also includes historic Fuerzas Populares de Liberación (FPL) leaders, Communist party officials, and members of Tony Saca's UNIDAD coalition, some of whom have had tense relationships with the United States. The U.S. government reportedly regards Sánchez Cerén's personal secretary, Manuel Melgar, as one of the people behind a 1985 attack on a café in San Salvador's Zona Rosa neighborhood that killed four U.S. marines.[13] Some U.S. officials may also have concerns about the decision to maintain David Múnguía Payés, the architect of the ill-fated 2012 gang truce who is under investigation for allowing arms trafficking by the military, as Minister of Defense.[14] The rest of the security cabinet is composed of FMLN politicians (Minister of Justice and Public Security Benito Lara) and/or police from the FMLN ranks (PNC director Mauricio Ramírez Landaverde).

Sánchez Cerén Biography

Born in 1944 in rural Quezaltepeque, El Salvador to a family of humble origin, Salvador Sánchez Cerén began his career as a teacher. He later transitioned from being a teacher's union leader to serving as a guerrilla commander for the Fuerzas Populares de Liberación or FPL during the war years. He was one of several FMLN leaders to sign the Peace Accords in 1992. Sánchez Cerén later served as a legislator from 2000-2008 before becoming Funes' Vice President and Minister of Education. Sánchez Cerén is generally regarded as more of a leftist than former President Funes and maintains close ties with Venezuela and Cuba. He also has a reputation for honesty and incorruptibility.

Many U.S. observers will be closely following the way in which President Sánchez Cerén manages his country's relationships with Cuba and especially Venezuela. While Cuba and the FMLN have a long history that predates the civil war, Venezuela has more recently provided significant economic investments in the country through entities associated with ALBA (the Bolivarian Alliance for the Peoples of Our America).[15] Early in the campaign, Sánchez Cerén said that he would join ALBA if elected.[16] While El Salvador has joined Venezuela's Petrocaribe[17] program in order to obtain energy supplies at lower costs, it is less certain how active his government will be in ALBA and how the future of both those entities will fare given Venezuela's precarious economic situation. Some observers have alleged that members of the FMLN close to Sánchez Cerén involved in ALBA are aligned with drug traffickers and the Revolutionary Armed Forces of Colombia (FARC), but those allegations have been disputed by other analysts.[18]

During his inaugural address, President Sánchez Cerén stressed the importance of transparency, conciliation, social justice, respect for the rule of law, and ensuring citizen security.[19] He said he aimed to boost growth and address the country's fiscal crisis through infrastructure projects and reforms to improve the business climate; continue investing in education and healthcare; and personally lead a National System of Citizen Security that will combat "organized crime, drug trafficking, extortions, and all expressions of violence." He did not refer to gangs or the truce. President Sánchez Cerén stressed the importance of actively working with the United States on the Partnership for Growth and promoting trade with Latin America, Asia, and Europe as well.

Constraints Facing the new Government

President Sánchez Cerén is likely to encounter some difficulty in implementing his government's priorities due to his country's severe fiscal constraints (discussed in the "Economic and Social Conditions" section below) and his party's lack of a congressional majority. His government already appears to be experiencing the same type of opposition to its proposals to raise taxes from the private sector and conservative parties in the National Assembly that the outgoing Funes Administration encountered. Those groups support austerity rather than higher taxes.

El Salvador's legislative branch is comprised of a unicameral National Assembly whose members are elected to serve for three-year terms. The current legislature was elected in March 2012 and will serve through April 2015. It is highly fragmented, with the FMLN holding 31 seats; ARENA, 28 seats; GANA,

11 seats; and several small parties holding the remaining 14 seats. The FMLN needs coalition partners in order to pass regular legislation requiring a simple majority. It will need broader support – three-quarters of the votes – in order to take on additional foreign debt. It remains to be seen whether President Sánchez Cerén will work as closely with the populist GANA party as President Funes did given the ideological differences between the two parties.

The Supreme Court of El Salvador is comprised of 15 justices that are divided among four chambers, including a constitutional chamber. Five justices are appointed to the Court every three years by a two-thirds vote in the National Assembly to serve for nine-year terms. Following the 2009 elections, the Assembly approved five new justices after difficult negotiations. Since their installation in 2009, the five justices on the constitutional chamber of the Supreme Court have taken actions which appeared intended to check the power of the president and the legislature, something it has historically failed to do. Analysts are waiting to see whether Sánchez Cerén will be willing to abide by the Court's decisions even if they are controversial and/or difficult to implement. This could prove to be extremely challenging should the court issue rulings limiting his executive authority or overturning past legislation, such as the country's 1993 Amnesty Law.

ECONOMIC AND SOCIAL CONDITIONS

El Salvador achieved stability and economic growth in the 1990s following its embrace of a "neoliberal" economic model that involved cutting government spending, privatizing state-owned enterprises, and, in 2001, adopting the U.S. dollar as its national currency. As expected, dollarization led to lower interest rates, low inflation, and easier access to capital markets, but it also took away the government's ability to use monetary and exchange rate adjustments to cushion the economy from external shocks. After posting strong growth rates in the 1990s, El Salvador's more moderate growth rates in the 2000s were not high enough to improve living standards among the Salvadoran people, approximately 47% of whom continued to live in poverty in 2010 (slightly lower than in 2001).[20] Emigration reduced unemployment and infused some households with income in the form of remittances, but also caused social disruptions.

The Funes government inherited a stagnating economy attracting little foreign direct investment (FDI) and mired in debt. El Salvador's already weak economy then contracted by 3.1% in 2009, largely as a result of the impact of the global financial crisis, U.S. recession, and damage wrought by Hurricane Ida. In March 2010, President Funes and the International Monetary Fund (IMF) agreed to a $790 million package premised on the idea that as the Salvadoran economy recovered, the government would strive to improve tax administration, restrict spending, and reallocate energy subsidies.[21] The IMF agreement paved the way for more than 1 billion dollars in loans from the World Bank and Inter-American Development Bank to support anti-poverty efforts, fiscal reform programs, and the creation of an export guarantee fund. Despite support from international donors, the Salvadoran economy has continued to perform poorly due to a combination of domestic and external factors.

Growth and Investment

Rather than presiding over a period of economic recovery, GDP growth averaged just 1.7% throughout the remainder of the Funes Administration, a rate too slow to spur progress in reducing poverty and inequality. Slow growth in the United States, El Salvador's top trade partner, likely weakened U.S. demand for Salvadoran exports and limited remittance flows. In addition, a tropical storm in 2011 caused more than $800 million in damage to roads, infrastructure, and agriculture and a coffee rust outbreak in 2013/2014 reduced production in that sector, one of El Salvador's main agricultural exports, by some 60%.[22] Still, economists have identified a lack of public and private (domestic and foreign) investment in the economy as the primary reason for the country's low growth rates.[23] Over the past decade or so, FDI in El Salvador has lagged behind other Central American countries and the Dominican Republic. The IMF and others have urged the country to adopt a whole series of reforms to attract investment, boost revenue, better target spending, and reduce the fiscal deficit.[24] The government may be able to continue issuing bonds and swapping expensive short-term debt for longer-term debt, but that is not a sustainable economic policy in the long run.

The Salvadoran government is seeking to attract foreign investment, particularly through public-private partnerships, to fund infrastructure development and is receiving U.S. support in that endeavor through the Partnership for Growth (PFG) initiative. The lack of foreign investment in El Salvador has been attributed to a number of factors, including the country's difficult business climate,[25] public security challenges, and a low-skilled labor force that is comparatively too expensive to compete with other low-cost producers. After consultations with the private sector, the Funes Administration tried to improve the country's legal and regulatory environment, combat extortion and other crimes that affect businesses, and align job training and education programs with private sector demands. A revised public-private partnerships (PPP) law that was enacted at the end of the Funes government could pave the way for President Sánchez Cerén's plans to modernize the airport, major ports, and certain highways.

Poverty

El Salvador's social challenges have been exacerbated by the country's long and violent civil conflict, persistent poverty and inequality, and family disintegration. As previously mentioned, the effects of the 2009 global financial crisis and U.S. recession set back some of the progress that had been made prior to that time in reducing poverty in the country. Nevertheless, conditional cash transfers and other social programs, largely supported by loans from multilateral development banks, helped reduce poverty between 2010 and 2013 from 47% to 41%.[26] Despite that progress, El Salvador's ranking in the U.N.'s Human Development Index (HDI) remained basically unchanged from the beginning to the end of the Funes government. El Salvador's ranking increased from 106 in 2009 to 107 in 2013. President Sánchez Cerén has stated his intention to increase social spending using revenues that should be made available by reductions in energy costs that will occur as a result of the country's recent entrance into Petrocaribe.[27]

SECURITY AND HUMAN RIGHTS

As with neighboring Honduras and Guatemala, El Salvador has been dealing with escalating homicides and generalized crime committed by gangs, drug traffickers, and other criminal groups. El Salvador recorded a homicide rate of 41.2 per 100,000 people in 2013, the fourth highest in the world.[28] El Salvador has the highest concentration of gang members per capita in Central America;[29] as a result, gangs, namely the Mara Salvatrucha (MS-13) and 18th Street gang,[30] are likely responsible for a higher percentage of homicides there than in neighboring countries. Drug trafficking organizations, including Mexican groups such as Los Zetas, have increased their illicit activities in El Salvador, including money laundering, albeit to a lesser extent than in

Honduras and Guatemala. Some analysts assert that connections between drug traffickers and the MS-13 gang are fairly well developed; others doubt that assertion.[31] President Sánchez Cerén mentioned the importance of combating organized crime and drug trafficking in his inaugural address, but did not refer to gangs specifically. He has since said that his government will not support a truce with organized crime groups.[32]

Amidst a climate of extreme violence and severe human rights abuses perpetrated by criminal groups, the State Department has reported that some Salvadoran military and police have been accused of involvement in unlawful killings and torture.[33] Abuses were common in the 2000s as successive ARENA government's launched aggressive "mano-dura" anti-gang policies.[34] El Salvador's Attorney General for human rights has begun investigating recent cases in which gang members may have been killed by paramilitary death squads; PNC officials have denied police involvement in those murders.[35] It will be a challenge for the Sánchez Cerén government to ensure that security officials (both police and military) do not engage in human rights abuses when carrying out law enforcement functions.

Police, Military, and Judicial Capabilities

In recent years, much has been written about the governance problems that have made El Salvador and other Central American countries susceptible to the influence of criminal elements and unable to guarantee citizen security. Resource constraints in the security sector have persisted over time as governments have failed to increase taxes. A lack of confidence in the underfunded public security forces has led many businesses and wealthy individuals in the region to turn to private security firms. As of 2013, El Salvador's Civilian National Police (PNC) had roughly 22,000 police while there were 28,600 private security guards working for firms in El Salvador.[36] Resource constraints aside, there have also been serious concerns about corruption in the police, prisons, and judicial system in El Salvador.

With more than 80% of the PNC budget devoted to salaries and benefits for current officers, there has historically been limited funding available for investing in training and equipment. According to the PNC's strategic plan for 2009-2014, the challenges it sought to overcome during the Funes government included "a lack of incentives and a career path for officers, deficient training and infrastructure, and a lack of intelligence capabilities, among others." Corruption, weak investigatory capacity, and an inability to prosecute officers accused of corruption and human rights abuses remain additional barriers to improved police performance.[37]

The PNC was restructured at least three times during the Funes Administration. The force began under the leadership of FMLN officials who prioritized crime prevention and internal reform, including an Inspector General who won praise from human rights organizations – and contempt from the Salvadoran Congress – for investigating PNC ties to organized crime.[38] Under pressure from Salvadoran society to reduce crime rates and reportedly from the U.S. government to replace then-Minister of Justice and Public Security Manuel Melgar because of concerns about his past role in the 1985 Zona Rosa killings, President Funes replaced the FMLN leadership at both the Ministry and the PNC with retired generals (David Munguía Payés and Francisco Salinas) in November 2011.[39] This angered human rights groups and the FMLN.

As Minister, David Munguía Payés removed most officers affiliated with the FMLN from leadership positions and appointed to key positions some officers who had been under investigation by the aforementioned Inspector General.[40] The arrest and hasty release of José Natividad Luna Pereira ("Chepe Luna"), a fugitive Salvadoran drug trafficker, in Honduras in August 2012 refocused scrutiny on Salvadoran police officers who had been under investigation for allegedly helping Luna evade capture in the past.[41] Munguía Payés' term will likely be remembered for his efforts to facilitate a gang truce that was criticized by some fellow officials, including El Salvador's Attorney General, and later abandoned by his successor.

In May 2013, the Salvadoran Supreme Court deemed that the reorganization of the Ministry and the PNC had violated the Peace Accords.[42] As a result, PNC leadership changed again as President Funes appointed a new Minister of Justice and Public Security and a new PNC director who were much more skeptical of the truce. Those leaders reportedly had good working relationships with their U.S. counterparts. According to the State Department, the PNC began to perform better in 2013 than it had in the recent past.[43]

Due to the weakness of the PNC and the severity of the security challenges the country is facing, El Salvador has deployed thousands of military troops to help the police carry out public security functions, without clearly defining when those deployments might end. As of April 2014, some 11,500 troops were involved in public security.[44] In April 2014, the Salvadoran Supreme Court upheld Funes' October 2009 decree that authorized the military to carry out police functions. Sánchez Cerén intends to keep the military engaged in public security efforts.

Few arrests carried out by PNC officials are successfully prosecuted in the Salvadoran justice system. The State Department maintains that "inefficiency, corruption, political infighting, and insufficient resources"[45] have hindered the performance of the Salvadoran judiciary. As Salvadoran police and prosecutors are often loathe to work together to build cases, few arrests lead to successful prosecutions. El Salvador's current criminal conviction rate is less than 5%. Delays in the judicial process and massive arrests carried out during prior anti-gang sweeps have resulted in severe prison overcrowding, with almost 27,000 prisoners being held in facilities designed to hold just over 8,000 inmates as of 2013. The State Department has described conditions in Salvadoran prisons and temporary holding cells as "harsh and life threatening."[46] Reducing prison overcrowding has become a key goal of U.S.-Salvadoran efforts.

Gang Truce[47]

When then-President Mauricio Funes appointed retired general Munguía Payés, as Minister of Justice and Public Security in November 2011, observers expected the minister to back a hardline approach to combating gangs. Munguía Payés did restructure the Salvadoran police and create a new elite anti-gang unit that has received U.S. training. However, he also lent government support to a former guerrilla fighter and deputy (who was his aid in the defense ministry) and a Catholic bishop who brokered a truce between the MS-13 and 18th Street gangs. In March 2012, Munguía Payés agreed to transfer high-ranking gang leaders serving time in prison to less secure prisons in order to facilitate negotiations between the gangs. Questions remain surrounding what exactly was negotiated with the gangs, when, and under what circumstances.[48] Munguía Payés denied his role in facilitating the truce until September 2012.[49]

Between the time the prison transfers took place and May 2013 (when Munguía Payés was removed from his post),[50] the Salvadoran government reported that homicide rates dramatically declined (from an average of roughly 14 per day to 5.5 per day). Gang leaders pledged not to forcibly recruit children into their ranks or perpetrate violence against women, turned in small amounts of weapons, and offered to engage in broader negotiations.[51] They did not agree to give up control of over their territories or stop extortions.

While some—including the Secretary General of the Organization of American States— praised the truce,[52] others expressed skepticism, maintaining that disappearances increased and extortions continued after it took effect.[53] El Salvador's Attorney General criticized the truce. After the Funes government withdrew its support for the truce mediators and reduced communication between imprisoned gang leaders and gang members in the streets in mid-2013, the truce began to unravel.[54] While some gangs reportedly tried to remain committed to the truce process despite the government's antagonism, factions of the 18th Street gang, and perhaps others groups as well, eventually ceased to abide by its principles.[55] By April 2014, average daily murder rates had risen to some 9 murders a day; gang attacks on police also occurred.[56] Gang leaders had previously predicted that murder rates could increase to 20 or 25 per day should the truce unravel completely; those predictions were born out by late May 2014.[57]

Confronting Past Human Rights Violations

As El Salvador seeks to deal with current security challenges posed by criminal groups in a way that respects human rights and the rule of law, the country is also still grappling with how to confront abuses committed during the country's civil conflict.

Twenty years after the U.N. Commission released its report on the war in El Salvador,[58] Amnesty International issued a statement lamenting that the perpetrators of crimes identified in that report had not been brought to justice in El Salvador and that survivors had not received reparations.[59] In October 2013, then-President Funes signed a decree creating a program to provide reparations to the victims of the armed conflict. It is unclear how much funding has been budgeted for that program and how many people it has assisted thus far, but human rights groups have urged President Sánchez Cerén to continue supporting its provision of social benefits to victims and their families.[60] In his inaugural address, Sánchez Cerén pledged to do so and to help families who are seeking to find out what happened to their loved ones. It is unclear whether he will urge the Salvadoran Supreme Court to overturn the 1993 Amnesty Law, as domestic and international human rights groups have been urging it to do.

Although the Amnesty Law makes bringing cases against human rights abusers from the war era nearly impossible to do in El Salvador, some former Salvadoran military leaders who have resided in the United States for more than a decade have faced judicial proceedings regarding their immigration statuses.[61] In recent years, the Human Rights Violators and War Crimes Unit within the Bureau of Immigration and Customs Enforcement (ICE) of the

Department of Homeland Security (DHS) has conducted investigations focused on human rights violations in El Salvador. In one case, Colonel Inocente Orlando Montano, one of the officials named by the Spanish judge as responsible for the aforementioned Jesuit murders, pled guilty to immigration fraud in September 2012; he has been sentenced to 21 months in prison and could then face extradition to Spain. ICE found that Montano had hidden his military past when applying for Temporary Protected Status (TPS) in the United States. In February 2014, a federal judge determined that a former Salvadoran Defense Minister, Gen. Carlos Eugenio Vides Casanova, can be removed (deported) based on his direct participation in brutal human rights violations. The judge ruled that Casanova "assisted or otherwise participated" in 11 violent incidents, including the 1980 killing of Archbishop Óscar Arnulfo Romero.[62]

U.S. RELATIONS

Despite dire predictions to the contrary, U.S. relations with the FMLN government of Mauricio Funes (2009-2014) remained friendly, although several Members of Congress raised concerns about corruption in the country during his term.[63] In March 2011, President Obama highlighted the importance of U.S.-Salvadoran relations by selecting El Salvador as the only Central American country to be included in his tour of Latin America. During that trip, he announced that El Salvador had been chosen as one of only four countries in the world deemed eligible to participate in the Partnership for Growth (PFG) initiative, a new foreign aid approach involving close collaboration between the United States and partner countries. El Salvador also completed a $461 million Millennium Challenge Corporation (MCC) compact during Funes' term.[64]

Obama Administration officials have pledged to continue economic and security cooperation under the PFG with President Sánchez Cerén and urged him to work with all of Salvadoran society to reach its goals, but questions remain about what types of policies he will adopt.[65] The MCC is likely to sign a second $277 million compact with the Sánchez Cerén government once certain conditions are met.[66] Security and governance issues are also likely to figure prominently on the bilateral agenda, particularly now that violent crime is trending upward.

Congress plays a key role in appropriating bilateral and regional aid to El Salvador, overseeing implementation of the Central American Regional

Security Initiative (CARSI), and consulting with the MCC on how El Salvador's second compact should proceed. Congress is likely to closely monitor how the government of Sánchez Cerén seeks to improve the investment climate in El Salvador, deal with the gang problem, and balance ties with the United States and relations with the governments of Venezuela and Cuba. Although U.S. officials have said that El Salvador's decision to join Petrocaribe would not impact bilateral relations, congressional concerns could arise should President Sánchez Cerén orient his foreign policy toward ALBA.[67]

Partnership for Growth Initiative

El Salvador is one of four countries that have been selected to participate in the Obama Administration's PFG Initiative, which seeks to foster sustained economic growth and development in top-performing low-income countries.[68] PFG involves greater collaboration between the donor and recipient countries than traditional U.S. assistance programs, but does not necessarily portend an increase in U.S. foreign aid. As a first step of implementing the PFG in El Salvador, a binational team conducted a diagnostic study, published in July 2011, which identified the two greatest constraints on growth in the country as crime and insecurity and a lack of competitiveness in the "tradables"[69] sector.[70] Those two concerns have become the focus of U.S. bilateral and regional programs in El Salvador.

On November 3, 2011, the two governments signed a 2011-2015 Joint Country Action Plan officially launching the PFG.[71] The Action Plan included detailed pledges by the U.S. and Salvadoran governments on how they intend to address the aforementioned growth constraints. Progress towards meeting each of 20 shared goals was to be mutually evaluated and then made public every six months. According to the plan, the U.S. government aims to help El Salvador address crime and insecurity by strengthening judicial sector institutions and supporting crime and violence prevention programs. The U.S. government also intends to help El Salvador improve its infrastructure (physical, human, and financial) and business climate in order to attract investment and boost competitiveness. Both governments aim to involve the private sector and other donors in the PFG. As such, former President Funes formed a Growth Council, composed of government and business officials, to improve public-private cooperation.

Two years into the implementation of the Joint Country Action Plan, the U.S. and Salvadoran governments reported in November 2013 that 17 of 20 bilateral goals were "on track" to being met.[72] However, issues such as promoting the use of extraditions as a crime control mechanism, maintaining good relations with the private sector, and attracting FDI in El Salvador had fallen behind schedule. Possibly due to the elections and impending change in government, a six-month scorecard was not released in May 2014. Since the last scorecard was released (November 2013), some goals have moved forward, including efforts to promote investment by enacting a more flexible public-private partnership law, while others have experienced setbacks. It is likely that the Action Plan and its priorities will be revised with the new government. Advances from the November 2013 and previous scorecards have included:

Reducing Crime and Insecurity: 1) the enactment of a freedom of information law, the approval of an asset forfeiture law, and the preparation of a civil service law; 2) the creation of a task force to combat crimes against small businesses and a task force to combat crime on public transit; and, 3) the expansion of temporary employment, training, and job placements programs for at-risk youth and the establishment of full-time schools nationwide.

Improving Productivity: 1) the approval of legislation backed by the private sector that is aimed at making it easier to invest in El Salvador and to better regulate the free trade zones; 2) the progress made in the Comalapa airport modernization project and the National Assembly approval of measures to support its financing; 3) the provision of job training and placement assistance by both governments that has helped more than 13,000 job seekers find employment; and, 4) the provision of U.S. trade capacity building assistance to over 3,400 businesses that have created 2,500 jobs since the PFG began, many of which are export-oriented.

It may take some time to discern whether the actions taken by each of the governments to achieve an "on track" ranking actually lead to tangible results. For example, in the security realm, are business owners' perceptions of the level of extortion they have to confront each day improving? Will the rate of reported extortions eventually decrease? Or, in the economic realm, how do investors rank the business climate in El Salvador? Is it improving? Will FDI increase?

Foreign Assistance

U.S. bilateral funding to El Salvador amounted to roughly $27.6 million in FY2013. El Salvador is receiving an estimated $22.3 million in U.S. aid in FY2014. Despite the austere U.S. budget environment, the Administration requested a slight increase to $27.6 million in bilateral assistance for El Salvador for FY2015 (see **Table 1**). Most other countries in Latin America and the Caribbean are slated to receive a cut in aid. Nevertheless, El Salvador receives less bilateral aid than neighboring Honduras and Guatemala.

Table 1. U.S. Bilateral Assistance to the El Salvador: FY2011-FY2015 (millions of dollars)

Account	FY2011	FY2012	FY2013	FY2014 (Estimate)	FY2015 (Request)
DA	23.9	23.9	21.4	19.3	25.0
ESF	0.0	2.0	3.4	0.0	0.0
FMF	1.3	1.3	1.7	1.9	1.6
GHP	3.1	0.0	0.0	0.0	0.0
IMET	1.5	0.0	1.1	1.1	1.0
NADR	0.0	1.0	0.0	0.0	0.0
TOTAL	29.8	29.2	27.6	22.3	27.6

Sources: U.S. Department of State, Congressional Budget Justification for Foreign Operations: FY2013-FY2015.

Notes: GHP= Global Health Program (includes total funds provided by the U.S. Agency for International Development and the State Department); DA=Development Assistance; ESF=Economic Support Fund; FMF=Foreign Military Financing; IMET=International Military Education and Training; NADR=Non-proliferation, Antiterrorism, Demining, and Related Programs.

As previously mentioned, since FY2013, U.S. bilateral assistance to El Salvador has been realigned to focus on reducing insecurity and boosting productivity in the country.[73] As part of that effort, the U.S. Agency for International Development (USAID) is increasing funding for institutional strengthening, violence prevention, and private sector competitiveness programs for municipalities and small and medium sized enterprises. In contrast, health programs have ended and education programs have been reoriented. USAID's education programs now focus on in-school and out-of-school youth in high-crime communities, while tertiary programs aim to align post-secondary training and education programs with current workforce demands.[74]

The Central American Regional Security Initiative[75]

In addition to bilateral aid, El Salvador receives assistance under the Central America Regional Security Initiative (CARSI, formerly known as Mérida-Central America), a package of counternarcotics and anticrime assistance for the region. As currently formulated, CARSI provides equipment, training, and technical assistance to build the capacity of Central American institutions to counter criminal threats. In addition, CARSI supports community-based programs designed to address underlying economic and social conditions that leave communities vulnerable to those threats. Since FY2008, Congress has appropriated nearly $806 million for Central America through Mérida/CARSI. The Obama Administration requested an additional $130 million for CARSI in FY2015. According to the Government Accountability Office (GAO), between FY2008 and FY2012, El Salvador received some $80.8 million in CARSI assistance (16% of the funds appropriated).[76]

Millennium Challenge Corporation[77]

First Compact Completed

In November 2006, El Salvador signed a five-year, $461 million compact with the Millennium Challenge Corporation (MCC) to develop its northern border region, where more than 53% of the population lives in poverty. The compact included (1) a $68.5 million **productive development project** to provide technical assistance and financial services to farmers and rural businesses; (2) an $89.1 million **human development project** to strengthen education and training and improve public services in poor communities; and (3) a $268.8 million **connectivity project** to rehabilitate the Northern Transnational Highway and some secondary roads.[78] The MCC compact was designed to complement the Dominican Republic-Central America-United States Free Trade Agreement (CAFTA-DR) and regional integration efforts and was expected to benefit more than 700,000 Salvadorans. It officially ended on September 20, 2012.

U.S. and Salvadoran officials have touted the MCC compact's effects on development and investment in El Salvador's northern border region. According to MCC, the compact enabled the construction or rehabilitation of 220 kilometers (137 miles) of roads and 23 bridges, which Salvadoran officials maintain has helped that area attract $57 million in private investment.[79] The project also provided electricity to 33,000 families; connected 7,634 households to potable water sources; created 15,250 jobs; and gave supplies and technical assistance to 17,467 small-scale producers.[80] The Salvadoran government complemented MCC investments in each of the project areas, investing $70 million in road construction and rehabilitation alone.

Critics have challenged these results. Some maintain that roads constructed by the MCC are falling apart due to design problems and a lack of maintenance.[81] Others criticized the project for providing only limited opportunities for community input in the compact development process and for failing to complete the entire infrastructure that was promised to local communities.[82]

Second Compact Still Pending

On December 15, 2011, the MCC Board announced that El Salvador would be eligible to develop a proposal for a second compact, and in February 2013 MCC obligated $3 million to assist El Salvador with compact development. On September 12, 2013, the MCC Board approved a second five-year compact with El Salvador, this time for $277 million; the Salvadoran government committed to match that contribution with $88 million in complimentary investments.[83] Key compact projects include:

- **Investment Climate Project ($42 million MCC funds/$50 million Salvadoran funds):** seeks to help the government develop and implement regulatory improvements and to better partner with private investors to build infrastructure and provide public services
- **Human Capital Project ($100.7 million MCC funds/$15 million Salvadoran funds):** supports full-day schooling, reforms to the policies and operations that govern teacher training and student assessment, and a new Technical, Vocational Education and Training system that is aligned with labor market demands
- **Logistical Infrastructure Project ($109.6 million MCC funds/$15.7 million Salvadoran funds):** will widen the part of El Salvador's coastal highway that connects the airport and the Ports of La Unión and Acajutla and improve border crossing facilities into Honduras at El Amatillo.

Although the MCC Board approved El Salvador's second compact in September 2013, it has yet to be signed. In response to some lingering concerns expressed by Board Members, the Salvadoran government designed a Priority Action Plan that was then agreed to by both governments to be completed prior to the compact's signing. The Action Plan required the Salvadoran government to 1) appoint a director and deputy director to a newly-established financial crimes investigation unit in the police; 2) approve an asset forfeiture law; 3) approve reformed anti-money laundering legislation that meets international standards; 4) approve reforms to the country's public private partnership law to make it attractive to investors; and, 5) issue a revised decree on how corn and bean seed are procured that is consistent with CAFTA-DR. In May 2014, U.S. Ambassador to El Salvador Mari Carmen Aponte stated that additional progress needs to be made in strengthening anti-money laundering legislation and in opening up El Salvador's seed procurement process to multinational companies in order for the compact to be signed.[84] Sánchez Cerén officials maintain that those issues are being resolved.[85]

Trade and CAFTA-DR[86]

The United States is El Salvador's main trading partner, purchasing 45% of its exports and supplying close to 39% of its imports.[87] Salvadoran exports to the United States include apparel, electrical equipment, sugar and coffee; its top imports from the United States are fuel oil, heavy machinery, and electrical machinery. Other main trade partners for El Salvador include: Guatemala, Honduras, and Mexico.

From the 1980s through 2006, El Salvador benefitted from preferential trade agreements, such as the Caribbean Basin Initiative and later the Caribbean Basin Trade Partnership Act (CBTPA) of 2000, which provided many of its exports, especially apparel and related items, duty-free entry into the U.S. market. As a result, the composition of Salvadoran exports to the United States has shifted from agricultural products, such as coffee and spices, to apparel and textiles.

On December 17, 2004, despite strong opposition from the FMLN, El Salvador became the first country in Central America to ratify the Dominican Republic-Central America-United States Free Trade Agreement (CAFTA-DR). El Salvador was also the first country to pass the agreement's required legislative reforms, implementing CAFTA-DR on March 1, 2006. Since that time, the volume of U.S.-Salvadoran trade has tended to follow trends in growth rates in the United States, with a variety of factors inhibiting the performance of Salvadoran exports vis-à-vis the other CAFTA-DR countries. Those factors have included a continued dependence on the highly competitive apparel trade, low levels of investment, public security problems, and broader governance concerns. As a comparison, El Salvador's exports to the United States increased from $2.0 billion in 2005 (the year before the agreement took effect there) to $2.4 billion in 2013. Nicaragua's exports increased from $1.1 billion in 2005 to $2.8 billion in 2013.

According to the July 2011 Partnership for Growth (PFG) assessment, a lack of competitiveness among firms in El Salvador that produce internationally traded goods has prevented the country from enjoying the full benefits of CAFTA-DR. The study found that El Salvador may be "missing eight percentage points of GDP compared to CAFTA colleagues" due to its productivity constraints. Low productivity may be due, in part, to the country's low level of human capital.

More recently, El Salvador and other Central American and Caribbean countries have become increasingly concerned about the potential impact of the Trans Pacific Partnership agreement (TPP) on their textile and apparel industries.[88] All things considered, tariff preferences provided through CAFTA-DR appear to be important in keeping apparel producers in those countries competitive in the U.S. market. A TPP agreement, if one is reached, has the potential to upset this situation. If apparel produced in Asian TPP countries gains duty-free access to the U.S. market, it could displace apparel manufactured with U.S. fabric in Central America, adversely affecting the textile and apparel industries in those countries and in the United States.

Counter-Narcotics Cooperation

Although El Salvador is not a producer of illicit drugs, it does serve as a transit country for narcotics, mainly cocaine and heroin, cultivated in the Andes and destined for the United States via land and sea. On September 13, 2013, President Obama included El Salvador on the annual list of countries designated as "major" drug-producing or "drug-transit" countries, for the third consecutive year.[89] A country's inclusion in the list does not mean that its antidrug efforts are inadequate. In 2013, Salvadoran officials seized 664 kilograms of cocaine and 908 kilograms of marijuana (roughly double what was seized in 2012), as well as $2.2 million in illicit cash. Still, corruption and inadequate manpower, training, and equipment continue to hinder El Salvador's antidrug efforts.[90]

U.S. assistance focuses on improving the interdiction capabilities of Salvadoran law enforcement and military agencies, particularly the joint military-police task force that was formed in 2012. It also supports the Attorney General's National Electronic Monitoring Center. Future U.S. support is going to be geared at helping implement El Salvador's recently passed asset forfeiture legislation and bolstering anti-money laundering efforts. The Obama Administration has recently named José Adán Salazar, a hotel magnate whom the Salvadoran government has yet to accuse of drug trafficking, as a major drug kingpin subject to U.S. sanctions.[91]

Comalapa International Airport in El Salvador serves as one of two cooperative security locations (CSLs) for U.S. anti-drug forces in the hemisphere. The CSL extends the reach of detection and monitoring aircraft into the Eastern Pacific drug smuggling corridors. Although the U.S. lease on the airport is set to expire in 2015, President-elect Sánchez Cerén indicated that he could support allowing the United States to continue using Comalapa for five more years in May 2014.[92] El Salvador is also the home of the U.S.-backed International Law Enforcement Academy (ILEA), which provides police management and training to officials from across the region.

Anti-Gang Efforts, the Designation of the MS-13 as a Major Transnational Criminal Organization, and U.S. Programs

Since the mid-2000s, several U.S. agencies have been actively engaged on the law enforcement and preventive side of dealing with Central American gangs; many U.S. anti-gang efforts in Central America began in El Salvador. In 2004, the Federal Bureau of Investigation (FBI) created an MS-13 Task Force to improve information-sharing and intelligence-gathering among U.S. and Central American law enforcement officials. The FBI established a vetted Transnational Anti-Gang Unit in El Salvador in 2007. In addition to arresting suspected gang members in the United States, ICE within DHS began coordinating its U.S. anti-gang efforts with its Transnational Criminal Investigative Unit activities in El Salvador.

Since FY2008, the State Department has funded anti-gang programs in El Salvador with support from the Mérida Initiative/Central American Regional Security Initiative (CARSI) and a line item in the Foreign Operations budget designated for "Criminal Youth Gangs" for which roughly $35 million was provided between FY2008 and FY2012. A Regional Gang Advisor based in El Salvador has coordinated Central American gang programs, including model police precincts and a school-based, law enforcement-led prevention program, since January 2008. USAID conducted a comprehensive gang assessment in 2005 and has since supported a variety of prevention programs for at-risk youth (including 39 outreach centers in El Salvador), municipal crime prevention projects, and community policing efforts. USAID-El Salvador has begun a $42 million public-private partnership focused on crime prevention and $2 million in grant awards to municipalities that have designed innovative crime prevention projects.

On October 11, 2012, the Treasury Department designated the MS-13 as a significant transnational criminal organization whose assets will be targeted for economic sanctions pursuant to Executive Order (E.O.) 13581.[93] Issued in July 2011 as part of the Obama Administration's National Strategy to Combat Transnational Organized Crime, E.O. 13581 enables the Treasury Department to block the assets of members and associates of designated criminal organizations and prohibit U.S. citizens from engaging in transactions with them.[94] Salvadoran officials seemed surprised by the designation, with then-President Funes asserting that U.S. officials may be "overestimating the economic risk or financial risk resulting from the criminal actions of the MS."[95] U.S. officials have stood by the designation, asserting that it will provide law enforcement with new tools to advance domestic and international anti-gang efforts.[96] At least six individuals have been designated as subject to U.S. sanctions.

In mid-2013, USAID suspended funding that was intended to reimburse the Salvadoran government for costs of a small grants program to assist individuals affected by the global financial crisis. Following media allegations that the benefits of the program were being directed to gang members, USAID investigated and found that the government's implementing agency had failed to follow correct program procedures, including how participating communities had been selected. For that reason, USAID ended its funding for that particular component, intended to benefit six of the "violence free" municipalities, before any funding had been reimbursed to the government for program costs. The Salvadoran government continued the program using non-U.S. government funding.[97]

Migration Issues

The United States is home to more than 1.9 million Salvadoran migrants.[98] Salvadorans comprise the 2nd largest foreign-born Hispanic population in the

United States (behind Mexico). In the 1980s, Salvadoran emigration was fueled by the country's civil conflict. Once that ended, family reunification, the search for economic opportunities, and periodic natural disasters fueled emigration. The movement of large numbers of poor Salvadorans to the United States has eased pressure on El Salvador's social service system and labor market while providing the country with substantial remittances that have constituted as much as 17% of the country's GDP.[99] On the other hand, emigration has arguably resulted in a "brain drain" of Salvadoran professionals, divided families, and left the economy reliant on remittances.

Temporary Protected Status

Following a series of earthquakes in El Salvador in 2001 and a determination that the country was temporarily incapable of handling the return of its nationals, the U.S. government granted Temporary Protected Status (TPS)[100] to an estimated 212,000 eligible Salvadoran migrants. TPS has been extended several times, and is currently scheduled to expire in March 2015.

Removals (Deportations)

The United States first began removing (deporting) large numbers of Salvadorans, many with criminal convictions, back to the region after the passage of the Illegal Immigrant Reform and Immigrant Responsibility Act (IIRIRA) of 1996.[101] Many contend that deportees who were members of the MS-13 and 18th Street gangs "exported" a Los Angeles gang culture to Central America and recruited new members from among the local populations. Removals from El Salvador have risen since the mid-2000s, with a significant percentage of those removed both then and now possessing some sort of criminal record, although not necessarily gang-related. As a comparison, in FY2004, DHS removed 6,342 Salvadorans from the United States, 42.5% of whom had criminal records.[102] In FY2012, DHS removed some 18,677 Salvadorans, 46.2% of whom had criminal records.[103]

The United States has been working with the Salvadoran government in a joint effort to improve the removal process. In December 2009, a bi-national working group consisting of migration authorities from both countries was formed in Washington, DC. Two of the group's goals were to expedite the process in order to avoid immigrants spending unnecessary time in U.S. detention centers and to address more general concerns about the current process; it is unclear whether those goals were met. As previously mentioned, El Salvador became the first country in the world to receive more complete criminal history information on U.S. gang deportees through the FBI's Criminal History Information Program (CHIP) in May 2012.[104] ICE expanded a Criminal History Information Sharing (CHIS) program that began in Mexico to El Salvador in 2014.[105] The CHIS program provides a criminal history on those removed from the United States with felony records to Salvadoran law enforcement. Salvadoran police would then reciprocate by exchanging similar information with U.S. officials on deportees who have serious criminal records in El Salvador.

Unaccompanied Alien Children[106]

Since 2011, several factors have contributed to a dramatic increase in unaccompanied alien children (UAC) immigrating from El Salvador (as well as Guatemala and Honduras) to the United States. Until recently, unaccompanied children had largely emigrated in search of opportunities (work and education) and/or to reunite with family living in the United States. Escalating crime and violence, as well as the government's inability to guarantee citizen security, have altered that tendency; 66% of the UAC from El Salvador interviewed by the U.N. High Commissioner for Refugees in 2013 had been abused or threatened by criminal actors.[107] Some minors are also reportedly emigrating in hopes of being granted asylum in the United States, or at least being temporarily released and reunited with family pending a U.S. immigration court hearing.[108] Flows of unaccompanied minors have increased even as the journey from Central America through Mexico to the United States has become more costly and more dangerous.

Addressing the root causes of why children are fleeing from El Salvador, how those children are treated once they arrive in the United States and the process by which they are repatriated – if applicable – are likely to be important issues on the bilateral migration agenda for the foreseeable future.[109] Vice President Joseph Biden focused on these topics, as well as the need to dissuade parents from sending their children illegally to the United States, at a meeting with President Sánchez Cerén and other Central American leaders held in Guatemala on June 20, 2014. Following that meeting, the Obama Administration announced the initiation of a five-year, $25 million crime and violence prevention program in El Salvador and the continuation of CARSI funding to address the root causes of migration.[110]

Neither the State Department nor USAID have funded large-scale assistance programs for repatriated Salvadorans. With State Department funding, the International Organization for Migration (IOM) implemented a two-phased small-scale program to assist in the repatriation of unaccompanied minors removed from the United State. The first phase, which was implemented in 2010, assisted in the reintegration of 52 children. The second phase, which was implemented in 2011, focused more on building Salvadoran government capacity to work with local communities and NGOs to support reintegration of unaccompanied repatriated minors rather than assisting large numbers of individuals.[111] The Obama Administration has announced its intention to provide $9.6 million to help El Salvador, Guatemala, and Honduras reintegrate repatriated migrants; the source of that funding was not specified.[112]

End Notes

[1] For historical background on El Salvador, see: Federal Research Division, The Library of Congress, *El Salvador: A Country Study*, ed. Richard Haggerty (Washington, DC: Library of Congress, 1990).

[2] Funes' election has been described as a watershed moment in the history of El Salvador. However, an analysis of Salvadoran voting behavior since 1992 concluded that Funes' victory occurred at least partially as a result of a gradual shift leftward among Salvadoran voters that was already evident by early 2008. Dinorah Azpuru, "The Salience of Ideology: Fifteen Years of Presidential Elections in El Salvador," *Latin American Politics and Society*, Summer 2010.

[3] "Interpol Panamá Pide Enviar Solicitud Extradición de Flores, Dice El Salvador," *EFE*, May 20, 2014.

[4] After Saca's term ended, ARENA dismissed him from the party for allegedly misappropriating party funds. Although Saca's personal wealth allegedly increased dramatically while he was in office, he has never been investigated for misappropriating public funds. Gabriel Labrador, "Ganancias de las Empresas de Saca se Multiplicaron Hasta Por 16 Cuándo Fue Presidente," *El Faro*, November 19, 2013.

[5] Priscilla B. Hayner, *Unspeakable Truths: Facing the Challenge of Truth Commissions*, (New York, NY: Routledge, 2002); Diana Villiers Negroponte, *Seeking Peace in El Salvador: The Struggle to Reconstruct a Nation at the End of the Cold War* (New York, NY: Palgrave Macmillan, 2012).

[6] Héctor Silva Ávalos, "Washington y El FMLN: Aprender a Bailar," *El Faro*, March 19, 2014.

[7] UCA, Instituto Universitario de Opinión Pública, *Los Salvadoreños y Salvadoreñas Evalúan al Gobierno de Mauricio Funes y el Pasado Proceso Electoral*, Press Bulletin Year 28, No. 3, May 2014.

[8] In addition to the El Mozote massacre, the 1989 killing of six Jesuit priests (five Spanish citizens), their housekeeper, and her daughter at the Universidad Centroamericana (UCA) marked another of the worst instances of human rights abuses carried out by military forces during the Salvadoran civil war. In 1991, under international pressure, a colonel, two lieutenants, a sub-lieutenant, and five soldiers were tried for the Jesuit murders. Only the colonel and one of the lieutenants were convicted; a 1993 amnesty law spared them significant prison time. It has prevented other high-level former military officials from being investigated or indicted in El Salvador for their alleged roles in the massacre. A Spanish

judge began investigating the massacre in 2009, however, based on the principle of universal jurisdiction for human rights abuses and the Spanish origin of five of the priests. On May 8, 2012, El Salvador's Supreme Court rejected Spain's request to have 13 former military officers allegedly involved in the murders extradited to stand trial.

[9] Daniel Valencia Caravantes and Efren Lemus, "La Idea de Crear una CICIG para El Salvador la Mató el Silencio del Presidente" *El Faro Sala Negra*, May 12, 2014.

[10] Fundación Salavdoreña para el Desarrollo Económico y Social (FUSADES), *Quinto año de Gobierno del Presidente Funes. Apreciación General*, May 2014.

[11] Linda Garrett, *El Salvador Update, March 2014*, Center for Democracy in the Americas (CDA), April 2, 2014.

[12] U.S. Department of State, "El Salvador Presidential Elections," Press Release, March 25, 2014.

[13] Tim Johnson, "El Salvador's Long-ago Civil War Still Colors U.S. Relations," *McClatchy Newspapers*, March 20, 2011.

[14] "El Salvador's Defense Minister Investigated for Arms Trafficking," *Latin News Daily Report*, June 11, 2014.

[15] ALBA is a block of countries that includes Bolivia, Cuba, Ecuador, Nicaragua, and a few Caribbean countries that receive government to government financial support from Venezuela. Alba Petróleos is a partnership between the Venezuelan state-owned oil enterprise PDVSA (60%) and an association of FMLN mayors (40%). The Venezuelan state provides generous long-term financing to Alba Petróleos on oil purchases. Alba Petróleos has used this financing to create a conglomerate with business holdings across a range of sectors.

[16] Antonio Soriano, "Primer Acto de Sánchez Sería Ingresar al ALBA," *El Mundo.com.sv*, January 12, 2013.

[17] Since 2005, the Venezuelan government has been providing oil to Central American and Caribbean nations at subsidized costs. Eoin O'Cinneide, "El Salvador Joins Petrocaribe," *Upstream*, June 3, 2014.

[18] Elliott Abrams, "Drug Traffickers Threaten Central America's Democratic Gains," *Washington Post*, January 3, 2014; Geoff Thale, "Response to Elliott Abrams' Op-Ed in the *Washington Post*,' *Washington Post*, January 13, 2014.

[19] "Discurso de Toma de Posesión de Salvador Sánchez Cerén," *La Página,* June 1, 2014.

[20] U.N. Economic Commission for Latin America and the Caribbean (ECLAC), *Social Panorama of Latin America, 2011*, December 2011.

[21] International Monetary Fund (IMF), "Press Release 10/95: IMF Executive Board Approves US$790 Million Standby Arrangement for El Salvador," March 17, 2010; IMF, *El Salvador: 2010 Article IV Consultation and First Review Under the Stand-By Arrangement*, IMF Country Report No. 10/307, October 2010.

[22] Famine Early Warning Systems Network, *The Coffee Sector in El Salvador is the Most Affected by the Coffee Rust Shock in Central America*, March 2014.

[23] Economist Intelligence Unit (EIU), *Country Report: El Salvador*, May 14, 2014.

[24] IMF, *IMF Executive Board Concludes 2013 Article IV Consultation with El Salvador*, May 22, 2013.

[25] El Salvador ranked lowest among the CAFTA-DR countries in the World Bank's 2013 Ease of Doing Business rankings. The World Bank, *Doing Business*, 2013.

[26] ECLAC, *Preliminary Overview of the Economies of Latin America and the Caribbean*, February 2014.

[27] Amadeo Cabrera et al. "El Salvador Ingreso a Acuerdo Petrocaribe," *La Prensa Gráfica*, June 3, 2014.

[28] UNODC, *Global Study on Homicide 2013: Trends, Contexts, Data*, March 2014.
[29] UNODC, *Transnational Organized Crime in Central America and the Caribbean: a Threat Assessment*, September 2012. Hereinafter, UNODC, September 2012.
[30] The 18th Street gang was formed by Mexican youth in the Rampart section of Los Angeles in the 1960s who were not accepted into existing Hispanic gangs. It was the first Hispanic gang to accept members from all races and to recruit members from other states. MS-13 was created during the 1980s by Salvadorans in Los Angeles who had fled the country's civil conflict. Both gangs later expanded their operations to Central America. For background, see: CRS Report RL34112, *Gangs in Central America*, by Clare Ribando Seelke.
[31] Douglas Farah and Pamela Phillips Lum, *Central American Gangs and Transnational Criminal Organizations*, International Assessment and Strategy Center, February 2013; UNODC, September 2012.
[32] "Sánchez Cerén Reafirma que no Dará Tregua al Crimen Organizado y la Violencia, *EFE*, June 10, 2014.
[33] U.S. Department of State, *Country Report on Human Rights Practices: El Salvador*, February 2014.
[34] *Mano dura* approaches have typically involved incarcerating large numbers of youth (often those with visible tattoos) for illicit association, and increasing sentences for gang membership and gang-related crimes. A *Mano Dura* law passed by El Salvador's Congress in 2003 was subsequently declared unconstitutional, but was followed by a *Super Mano Dura* package of anti-gang reforms in July 2004. These reforms enhanced police power to search and arrest suspected gang members and stiffened penalties for convicted gang members, although they provided some protections for minors accused of gang-related crimes. Most youth arrested under *mano dura* provisions were subsequently released for lack of evidence that they committed any crime.
[35] James Bargent, "Has Gang Violence in El Salvador Sparked a Death Squad Revival?," *Insight Crime*, May 23, 2014.
[36] Red de Seguridad y Defensa de América Latina (RESDAL), *Índice de Seguridad Pública y Ciudadana en América Latina: El Salvador*, 2013.
[37] U.S. Department of State, *Country Report on Human Rights Practices: El Salvador*, February 2014; Héctor Silva Ávalos, *Infiltrados: Crónica de la Corrupción en la PNC (1992-2013)*, (San Salvador: UCA Editores, 2014).
[38] "Comisión Especial Cita a Inspectora Zaira Navas," *El Diario de Hoy*, September 21, 2010.
[39] "Presidencia Informa que Manuel Melgar Dejó Ministerio de Seguridad," *El Faro*, November 8, 2011.
[40] Ibid.
[41] Adriana Beltrán, "Release of Suspected Drug Trafficker in Honduras Raises Questions about Corruption in Honduras and El Salvador," Washington Office on Latin America (WOLA), August 10, 2012.
[42] Sonja Wolf, "Policing Crime in El Salvador," NACLA Report on the Americas, Spring 2012.
[43] U.S. Department of State, Bureau of International Narcotics and Law Enforcement Affairs, *2014 International Narcotics Control Strategy Report*, March 2014. Hereinafter: *INCSR*, March 2014.
[44] "SC Provides Security Boost for Sánchez Cerén in El Salvador," *Latin News Daily Report*, April 14, 2014.
[45] U.S. Department of State, *Country Report on Human Rights Practices: El Salvador*, February 2014.
[46] Ibid.

[47] For background, see: CRS Report RL34112, *Gangs in Central America*, by Clare Ribando Seelke.

[48] "MS Tenía una Computadora Oculta en el Penal de Gotera," *El Salvador.com*, February 18, 2014; Carlos Martínez, "Los dos Versiones de Nelson Rauda Sobre la Tregua," *El Faro*, February 17, 2014.

[49] Carlos Martínez and Jose Luis Sanz, "The New Truth About the Gang Truce," *Insight Crime*, September 14, 2012.

[50] In May 2013, El Salvador's Supreme Court nullified President Funes' appointment of retired general David Munguía Payés as Minister of Justice and Public Security because it contravened the Peace Accords and a constitutional provision stipulating that public security must be led by an individual independent of the military. Munguía Payés' replacement, Ricardo Perdomo, has opposed the truce.

[51] WOLA, *El Salvador's Gang Truce: In Spite of Uncertainty, an Opportunity to Strengthen Prevention Efforts*, July 17, 2012; Randal C. Archibold, "Gangs' Truce Buys El Salvador a Tenuous Peace," *New York Times*, August 27, 2012.

[52] Eric Sabo, "Gang Truce Spurs Bond Rally as El Salvador's Murders Drop 70%," *Bloomberg*, July 23, 2012.

[53] Douglas Farah, *The Transformation of El Salvador's Gangs into Political Actors*, Center for Strategic & International Studies (CSIS), June 21, 2012.

[54] "Gang Violence Peaks Again in El Salvador," *Latin News Daily*, December 18, 2013.

[55] "Presidente de El Salvador Dice que "Mara 18" Rompió la Tregua entre Pandillas," *Agencia EFE*, April 26, 2014.

[56] Zlatica Hoke, "Criminal Gangs in El Salvador Return to War Path After Two-Year Truce," *Voice of America*, March 25, 2014; Grant Hurst, "Increases in Salvadoran Gang Activity and use of Automatic Firearms Raise Death, Injury, and Collateral Damage Risks," *IHS Global Insight Daily Analysis*, April 22, 2014.

[57] Carlos Martinez and José Luis Sanz, "Para que la Gente nos Crea Estamos Dispuestos a Dejar de Meter Jóvenes a la Pandilla," *El Faro*, January 27, 2014; Carlos Martinez and José Luis Sanz, "How El Salvador's Security Ministry Dismantled Truce, Unleashed Mayhem," *Insight Crime*, May 28, 2014.

[58] Belisario Betancur, Reinaldo Figueredo Planchart, and Thomas Buergenthal, *From Madness to Hope: The 12-Year War in El Salvador: Report of the Commission on the Truth for El Salvador*, United Nations, 1993.

[59] Amnesty International, "El Salvador: No Justice 20 Years on from UN Truth Commission," press release, March 15, 2013.

[60] Teresa Alvarado, "Organizaciones Piden al Presidente Electo Continuar con Reparación a Víctimas de la Guerra," *Transparencia Activa*, March 21, 2014.

[61] Julia Preston, "Salvadoran May Face Deportation for Murders," *New York Times*, February 23, 2012. ICE, "Former Salvadoran Military Officer Pleads Guilty to Concealing Information From U.S. Government," press release, September 11, 2012. For more pending cases, see: http://cja.org/article.php?list=type&type=199.

[62] Julia Preston, "Salvadoran General Accused in Killings Should Be Deported, Miami Judge Says," *New York Times*, April 11, 2014.

[63] See, for example, "Statement of Senator Patrick Leahy on Funding for a Second Millennium Challenge Compact for El Salvador," press release, September 18, 2013. Hereinafter: Leahy, 2013.

[64] Established in 2004, the Millennium Challenge Corporation (MCC) provides economic assistance through a competitive selection process to developing nations that demonstrate

positive performance in three areas: ruling justly, investing in people, and fostering economic freedom.

[65] U.S. Department of State, "El Salvador Presidential Elections," press release, March 25, 2014; U.S. Embassy in El Salvador, "Discurso de la Embajadora de los Estados Unidos Mari Carmen Aponte en el Desayuno de la Cámara Americana," press release, April 24, 2014.

[66] Amadeo Cabrera, "FMLN Cede a Reformas Ley Lavado y Cumplir TLC," *La Prensa Gráfica*, May 22, 2014.

[67] Diana Arias, "Ingreso a Petrocaribe no Disolverá la "Relación Sólida" Entre EE.UU. y El Salvador," *La Página*, June 2, 2014.

[68] The principles behind the PFG Initiative are to (1) focus on broad-based economic growth; (2) select countries with demonstrated performance and political will; (3) use joint decision-making and prioritization of activities; (4) support catalytic policy change and institutional reform; (5) leverage U.S. government engagement for maximum impact; and (6) emphasize partnership and country ownership. The other PFG countries are Ghana, the Philippines, and Tanzania.

[69] "Tradables" refers to products that are or can be traded internationally.

[70] U.S. Department of State, *Partnership for Growth: El Salvador Constraints Analysis*, July 19, 2011.

[71] U.S. Department of State, *Partnership for Growth: El Salvador-United States Joint Country Action Plan 2011-2015*, November 2011, http://photos.state.gov/libraries/elsavador/92891/octubre2011/Joint_Country_Action_Plan.pdf.

[72] U.S. Department of State, *Partnership for Growth El Salvador-United States, Six Month Scorecard: May 2013- November 2013.*

[73] U.S. Department of State, *FY2013 Congressional Budget Justification for Foreign Operations.*

[74] U.S. Department of State, *FY2015 Congressional Budget Justification for Foreign Operations.*

[75] CRS Report R41731, *Central America Regional Security Initiative: Background and Policy Issues for Congress*, by Peter J. Meyer and Clare Ribando Seelke.

[76] GAO, Central America: *U.S. Agencies Considered Various Factors in Funding Security Activities, but Need to Assess Progress in Achieving Interagency Objectives*, GAO-13-771, September 25, 2013, available at: http://gao.gov/assets/660/658145.pdf.

[77] See: CRS Report RL32427, *Millennium Challenge Corporation*, by Curt Tarnoff.

[78] The Compact also included $28 million for program administration and $6 million for monitoring and evaluation.

[79] Ambassador of El Salvador to the United States Francisco Altschul, "Salvadoran Ambassador Francisco Altschul: The Case for a new MCC Compact with El Salvador," *The Hill*, October 1, 2012.

[80] Millennium Challenge Corporation (MCC), "El Salvador: Table of Key Performance Results," November 10, 2012.

[81] Carlos Hernández, "Conductores Denuncian Deterioro de Carretera Longitudinal Norte," *La Página,* December 24, 2013.

[82] "¿Fomilenio: Misión Cumplida?" *Editorial UCA*, September 21, 2012.

[83] MCC, *Congressional Notification*, September 19, 2013.

[84] Loida Martínez Avelar, "Aún no Resuelven Trabas para Firma de FOMILENIO II," *La Prensa Gráfica*, May 21, 2014.

[85] Amadeo Cabrera, "FMLN Cede a Reformas Ley Lavado y Cumplir TLC," *La Prensa Gráfica*, May 22, 2014.

[86] For historical background, see: CRS Report R42468, *The Dominican Republic-Central America-United States Free Trade Agreement (CAFTA DR): Developments in Trade and Investment*, by J. F. Hornbeck.

[87] Trade data contained in this section are from Global Trade Atlas.

[88] CRS Report R42772, *U.S. Textile Manufacturing and the Trans-Pacific Partnership Negotiations*, by Michaela D. Platzer.

[89] The White House, Office of the Press Secretary, "Presidential Determination on Major Illicit Drug Transit or Major Illicit Drug Producing Countries for Fiscal Year 2014," press release, September 14, 2013.

[90] *INCSR*, March 2014.

[91] "Estados Unidos Designa a José Adán Salazar Como Capo de la Droga," *La Prensa Gráfica*, May 31, 2014.

[92] "Sánchez Cerén Mantendrá Base de Vigilancia Antidrogas EE.UU. en El Salvador," *EFE*, May 14, 2014.

[93] The criteria established for declaring a transnational criminal organization pursuant to Executive Order 13581 are available at: http://www.whitehouse.gov/the-press-office/2011/07/25/executive-order-blocking-property-transnationalcriminal-organizations. U.S. Department of Treasury, "Treasury Sanctions Latin American Criminal Organization," press release, October 11, 2012.

[94] The first four criminal organizations that received Transnational Criminal Organization (TCO) designations were: the Brother's Circle, the Camorra, Los Zetas, and the Yakuza. See: The White House, Office of the Press Secretary, Executive Order 13581--Blocking Property of Transnational Criminal Organizations," July 25, 2011.

[95] Geoffrey Ramsey, "El Salvador President: US 'Overestimating' MS-13," *InSight Crime*, October 11, 2012.

[96] Garrett, October 2012.

[97] Teresa Alvarado, "FISLD Continuará Financiando Programa PATI en Municipios Excluidos por USAID," *Transparencia Activa*, September 13, 2013.

[98] Anna Brown and Eileen Patten, *Statistical Portrait of the Foreign-Born Population in the United States, 2012*, April 2014.

[99] U.S. Department of State, *Partnership for Growth: El Salvador Constraints Analysis*, July 19, 2011.

[100] See: CRS Report RS20844, *Temporary Protected Status: Current Immigration Policy and Issues*, by Ruth Ellen Wasem and Karma Ester.

[101] IRIRA expanded the categories of illegal immigrants subject to deportation and made it more difficult for immigrants to get relief from removal.

[102] DHS, Office of Immigration Statistics, *2004 Yearbook of Immigration Statistics*.

[103] DHS, Office of Immigration Statistics, *2012 Yearbook of Immigration Statistics*.

[104] U.S. Department of State, Embassy in San Salvador, "El Salvador Signs CHIP," May 9, 2012.

[105] U. S. Embassy in San Salvador, "U.S. and El Salvador Share Criminal and Migratory Information," press release, May 15, 2014.

[106] For an examination of the domestic response to the increase in child migrants and U.S. immigration policy, see: CRS Report R43599, *Unaccompanied Alien Children: An Overview*, by Lisa Seghetti, Alison Siskin, and Ruth Ellen Wasem.

[107] U.N. High Commissioner for Refugees (UNHCR), *Children on the Run: Unaccompanied Children Leaving Central America and Mexico and the Need for International Protection*, May 2014.

[108] Julia Preston, "Hoping for Asylum, Migrants Strain U.S. Border," *New York Times*, April 10, 2014; Jennifer Scholtes, "CBP Chief: Policies may be Fueling Spike in Minors Crossing Border Illegally," *CQ News*, April 2, 2014.
[109] Jennifer Scholtes and Emily Ethridge, "Alone, Illegal, and Underage: the Child Migrant Crisis," *Roll Call*, May 28, 2014.
[110] The White House, Office of the Press Secretary, "Fact Sheet: Unaccompanied Children from Central America," press release, June 20, 2014.
[111] IOM. *Final Reports to the Government of the United States of America: Return and Reintegration of Unaccompanied Minors*, 2010, 2011.
[112] The White House, Office of the Press Secretary, "Fact Sheet: Unaccompanied Children from Central America," press release, June 20, 2014.

In: El Salvador
Editor: Joelle Foster

ISBN: 978-1-63321-766-9
© 2014 Nova Science Publishers, Inc.

Chapter 2

PARTNERSHIP FOR GROWTH EL SALVADOR-UNITED STATES, SIX MONTH SCORECARD: NOVEMBER 2013-MAY 2014[*]

U.S. Department of State

OVERVIEW

Constraint 1: Crime and Insecurity	Score May 2014
1. Strengthen Justice Sector Institutions	On Track
2. Improve Criminal Justice Procedures	On Track
3. Reduce Impact of Crime on Businesses	On Track
4. Reduce Impact of Crime on Commuters/Public Transportation	On Track
5. Remove Assets from Criminal Organizations	On Track
6. Strengthen El Salvador's Civil Service	On Track
7. Promote a National Dialogue to Improve Security	On Track
8. Assist At-Risk Youth Through Economic Opportunities	On Track
9. Strengthen the PNC	On Track
10. Improve Education Opportunities for Youth in High-Risk Municipalities	On Track

---

[*] This is an edited, reformatted and augmented version of report issued May 2014.

(Continued)

11. Prevent Crime & Violence in Key Municipalities and Support Reforms	On Track
12. Reduce Overcrowding in Prisons	Behind Schedule
13. Enhance the Security of the Prisons	Behind Schedule
14. Promote use of Extradition to Combat Crime	On Track
Constraint 2: Low Productivity in the Tradables Sector	
1. Establishment of a Growth Council	On Track
2. Reduce Firms' Cost to Improve Their Competitiveness	On Track
3. Strengthen Labor Force to Match Labor Market Demand	On Track
4. Raise (Net) Tax Revenue by 2015	On Track
5. Support a Strategy for Attracting & Promoting Foreign Direct Investment	Behind Schedule
6. Surmount Low Productivity in Tradables	On Track

CONSTRAINT 1: CRIME AND INSECURITY

Goal 1-2: Professionalize and improve the effectiveness of justice sector institutions (procedures and practices) to increase their ability to combat crime and insecurity in El Salvador, as well as enhance the public perception of these government institutions.	On Track

Goal 1 - The U.S. Government (USG) and the Government of El Salvador (GOES) continue joint efforts to build effective criminal justice sector institutions, developing strong professionals, modern systems, and standardized procedures to combat crime. A new training facility, recently inaugurated in San Miguel, provides prosecutors in eastern El Salvador the skills needed to prepare and deliver sound, evidence-based cases to help reduce impunity. The Public Defender's Office now has a training plan for public defenders, and 69 justice sector officials completed two courses on leadership and organizational change to promote efficiency and customer service. In a study tour to Costa Rica, sponsored by the USG, Supreme Court officials gained first-hand knowledge on best practices and management of effective anticorruption offices. During this scorecard period, the USG provided assistance to the Judicial Council for the design of a training program and a merit-based system for the evaluation and selection of judges, a major PFG goal. To improve police efficiency, the USG also provided support to the National Civilian Police (PNC) in preparing an operations manual for the newly created Secretariat of Planning and International Coordination and a plan for strengthening the Internal Affairs Unit of the PNC's Inspector General's Office.

Goal 2 - To improve coordination among justice sector institutions and to promote citizen participation, the USG and the GOES established a justice sector working group that includes civil society and another working group on transparency and anti-corruption. The GOES, with USG support, is improving services for victims of domestic and sexual violence. Three new victims assistance centers were established during this scorecard period in the San Miguel Attorney General's Office, the Sensuntepeque Police Delegation, and the Cojutepeque Public Defender's Office, bringing the total to 11 centers nationwide. These facilities are now fully equipped and staffed to provide victims with humane treatment and complete services, including psychological counseling and accompaniment through all legal proceedings, which helps reduce the number of victims who abandon their cases. Personnel at the centers have been trained in victim assistance and investigation of crimes related to gender-based violence. During this period, 1,657 victims were attended at these centers. The USG also supported the Attorney General's Office in establishing two specialized offices to process criminal cases under streamlined procedures in the Zacatecoluca and Ilobasco Prosecutor's offices. The Chief of Police and Attorney General approved the establishment of 14 new joint police-prosecutor investigative teams to undertake and facilitate criminal investigations at the department level.

Goal 3: Reduce the impact of organized crime on small and medium businesses, potentially the most dynamic sector of the economy, whose contribution to growth is key to the economic well-being of El Salvador.	On Track

The Business Crimes Task Force (BCTF) is now a fully functioning and operational investigative unit. It has conducted over 27 investigations, of which four are completed. These four investigations resulted in 17 arrests; nine of the arrestees were convicted on extortion-related offenses, and the remaining eight are currently awaiting trial. The BCTF has conducted over 50 undercover operations and has seized several motor vehicles, a firearm, and numerous communications devices. The Task Force is utilizing sophisticated investigative techniques to transition from simple extortion cases to complex investigations designed to identify and dismantle the command and control structure of criminal enterprises. To improve unit efficiency the USG has trained the BCTF in investigative techniques, interview techniques, analysis, surveillance, undercover operations, and personal defense. In addition, the USG has identified and provided equipment needed to achieve the GOES's goals and objectives. Task Force representatives continue to partner with the National Commission for Micro and Small Businesses (CONAMYPE) to provide small and medium businesses with information on the BCTF and extortion prevention.

Goal 4: Facilitate economic growth by ensuring El Salvador's labor force is protected from crime while transiting to and from work, and ensuring that the public transportation service providers serving the labor force are protected from crime.	On Track

The Public Transportation Task Force has started investigating public transportation crime cases and will become a formal unit in the PNC. All police and prosecutors in the unit have been vetted. A procedures manual for the Task Force was drafted and a training plan was initiated to improve investigation and interview techniques, analysis and surveillance, and personal defense. In addition, the GOES continues to improve the transparency and accountability of the Vice Ministry of Transportation (VMT). The VMT's Transparency Office, established with USAID assistance, is now fully functioning and to date 129 of a total of 130 requests for information have been fulfilled. The VMT is also updating its procedures manual to reduce corruption and improve efficiency. A citizen oversight group, monitoring the transparency of the Ministry of Public Works' construction of the new Integrated System of Public Transportation in the Metropolitan Area (SITRAMSS) delivered its final report to the authorities, with recommendations for improvement.

Goal 5: Remove assets from criminal organizations and fund and support security programs through the use of seized property and	On Track

The new Asset Forfeiture Law was enacted in November 2013 and will take effect in June 2014. Bylaws were drafted by the Ministry of Justice and Public Security. INL and Treasury OTA coordinated technical assistance in the drafting of the bylaws. The proposed bylaws are expected to be approved by the President in June 2014. INL sponsored two workshops in February and March 2014 to assist with the application of the new law. The ten-member Rule of Law team, created by the Technical Secretary of the President, also received training and mentoring in understanding and applying the new Asset Forfeiture Law. This included GOES representatives from Treasury, the Armed Forces, the Attorney General's office, the Ministry of Justice and Public Security, Customs, and the National Civilian Police. In addition, INL sponsored training and mentoring for 31 judges who are potential candidates for the new asset forfeiture tribunals and met with 19 members of Foundation *Transparencia*, a Salvadoran NGO that assists the GOES on transparency issues. The meeting and workshops served to increase understanding and encouraged application of the new law.

Goal 6: Professionalize El Salvador's civil service and enhance public confidence in the government.	On Track

The final draft bill for a new civil service law was delivered to the Presidency's Strategic and Legal Affairs Secretariats. The draft bill was also reviewed by the International Labor Organization (ILO) for to assure consistency and compliance with international labor treaties ratified by El Salvador. The ILO's technical opinion and comments were positive, however the GOES has announced that additional consultations are necessary before submitting the bill to the Legislative Assembly. A communications strategy and materials for an awareness campaign for public employees and the general population on the benefits of civil service reform was finalized with USG assistance and will be implemented during the next scorecard period. The Institute of Access to Public Information (IAIP) is operating from its USG-equipped facilities, with a staff of 35 people. Since opening, the IAIP has managed 160 procedures (128 appeals and 32 complaints), of which 110 have been resolved. The USG provided technical assistance for the creation of the IAIP's website, launched on April 3. Since the Access to Public Information Law entered into effect, 30,500 requests for information have been received, with 98 percent of them fulfilled within 4.5 days of filing. A fourth group of 45 information officers and other GOES employees began the "Access to Information and Transparency" certificate course. During this period, the "open government" website, containing 51,000 documents for public access, reported 61,641 visits. The "useful information" website, which hosts 33 databases of public information, reported 641,090 visits. The USG provided technical assistance and equipment for these web-based transparency tools.

Finally, 100 new citizen committees were established to monitor the implementation of the "School Food and Health Program" in public schools in the municipalities of Quezaltepeque, Lourdes Colón, Jayaque, Sacacoyo, Talnique, and Tepecoyo.

Goal 7: Promote a national dialogue on actions to improve citizen security in El Salvador. Actively involve all sectors of national life, including the private sector, the media, nongovernmental organizations, churches, etc., in efforts to solve the problem of insecurity.	On Track

The USG and GOES continue to implement a joint communications strategy to promote discussion of PFG efforts to improve citizen security in El Salvador. This includes press outreach, publication of articles on PFG and security issues, websites in English and Spanish, access to official PFG documents and sharing of information on actions taken to address PFG goals under the security constraint. The GOES and USG, with private sector support and participation, organized a public fair to celebrate the second anniversary of PFG in December 2013. During the day-long event, held at a popular San Salvador shopping mall, over 1,500 people visited stands and learned about the partnership between the USG and GOES to combat crime and increase economic growth in El Salvador. The fair received ample media coverage, including a front page article with pictures in *La Prensa Grafica* newspaper. Two other major public events, the launch of violence prevention plans in 13 municipalities, and the visit of a group of Salvadoran mayors to Colombia to learn about crime and violence prevention activities, were widely publicized. The number of public events was reduced temporarily, due to restrictions required by electoral law during the presidential election. Meetings of Municipal Crime Prevention Councils, which are supported directly by the USG, continued to take place to define local action plans. The Government of El Salvador launched a complementary effort for rehabilitation and reinsertion of youth in seven municipalities, known as the Commissions for Municipal Dialogue. The Ministry of Justice and Public Security continued to organize monthly fora on public security at the local (department) level. The President and Minister of Justice and Public Security continued to meet with various sectors of society to promote a national consensus on crime prevention and public security.

Goal 8: Assist at-risk youth between ages 16-25 through efforts to afford them economic opportunities and engage them in productive activities.	On Track

During this period, 446 youth who received vocational training by the USG obtained employment or started a micro-enterprise. Through another program, the USG trained 289 youth and provided start-up funds to 106 participants for microenterprises. A GOES temporary employment program, supported by the USG, trained over 2,250 primarily urban youth beneficiaries in job and life skills. Under the San Salvador Metropolitan Area Project's "Pact for Security and Employment," the GOES trained 70 youth in Soyapango and Ilopango in starting micro-enterprises and provided seed capital. The GOES inaugurated a youth penitentiary that offers vocational training, including carpentry, metalwork, tailoring, handicrafts, and agriculture for youth rehabilitation. Additionally, the GOES is beginning two pilot social and economic inclusion projects for at-risk youth, supported by other international donors, with activities in San Vicente, Cojutepeque, San Pedro Perulapán, Zacatecoluca, and Ciudad Delgado. The GOES's National Strategy for Violence Prevention, launched in February, includes youth as a target group for prevention activities.

Goal 9: Support the PNC to strengthen its service orientation as a means for violence prevention and effective crime control with a focus on building leadership skills within the police force and on improved relationships between police and communities.	On Track

The USG continues to strengthen relations between police and the communities they serve by expanding the Gang Resistance Education and Training (GREAT) program. Thirty-six new officers were certified as instructors for the program and three PNC GREAT-certified instructors, selected for the GREAT "Train the Trainer" program, have completed two of the three phases for joining the GREAT international training team. The GREAT program has expanded into the communities of San Martin, La Herradura de La Paz, and San Salvador. The USG also awarded a $100,000 grant to expand the PNC Police Athletic League in Santa Ana and in La Herradura de La Paz, which will benefit approximately 1,000 at-risk youth. Approximately 8,000 students are receiving training under the GREAT program since January 2014. The USG completed a baseline public opinion and crime statistics survey for the police model precinct in Usulutan. During this reporting period, four new community policing programs were established in the municipalities of Jiquilisco, Ciudad Barrios, Puerto La Libertad, and Chalchuapa, including the development of community policing action plans and the training of 490 police officers in the basic Community Policing course. The USG also supported the PNC in providing follow-up training for 1,074 police officers in 12 previously established community policing localities. To strengthen community-police relations, the USG sponsored 1,225 students, parents, and community members in joint activities with the police, such as community forums, sporting events, vocational instruction and fairs, summer school activities, street theatre productions, and more.

Goal 10: Improve educational opportunities for in-school and out-of-school youth in targeted high risk municipalities with high crime rates. The USG is dedicated to supporting the Ministry of Education in implementation of their "Social Education Plan" and the GOES' "Five Year Plan" by focusing efforts on the four areas of concern described in the plan.	On Track

The Ministry of Education (MOE) continues to advance the Full Time Inclusive School (SI-EITP) approach. This model promotes community participation, inclusion, and creative learning methodologies and integrates available resources in the community to enhance quality education. As a result of collaboration between the MOE, World Bank, USG and Italian Cooperation, the model has been expanded to 1,500 schools in 59 municipalities. This joint effort has reached over 400,000 students, 13,000 teachers, and 1,500 principals. Of this total, the USG expanded its work to 18 high-risk municipalities providing services to 125,000 students in 411 schools, and trained 600 teachers, 290 principals, and 201 MOE officials in new teaching methodologies and tools and strategies for implementing the SI-EITP model. The USG also expanded crime prevention activities to promote safe schools, reaching over 53,300 students, and expanded activities for over 1,800 out-of-school youth to encourage them to return to formal education. A workshop was organized by the MOE and international donors on "Building the Country's Commitment to Quality and Inclusive Education." This was the first event implemented jointly by donors to raise awareness and commitment to the expansion of the SI-EITP model. The workshop was attended by over 100 people, including civil society and private sector representatives, academic institutions, and government. Under the "Adopt-a-School" program, 43 new public-private partnerships were established with USG support, training 2,003 teachers and 158 principals to improve the quality of education for 129,439 students in 115 schools.

Goal 11: Prevent crime and violence in key municipalities of El Salvador and support reforms, as outlined on components 2 (Social Prevention of Violence and Crime) and 5 (Institutional and Legal Reform) of the National Policy for Justice, Public Safety and Violence Prevention.	On Track

The GOES launched the National Violence Prevention Strategy (ENPV) in February, representing a significant step in violence prevention. Subsequently, the GOES carried out 35 training workshops to disseminate the strategy to 636 members of Municipal Violence Prevention Committees (CMPV) and Departmental Management Cabinets. GOES vocational training sessions benefitted 125 youth from the five municipalities most affected by violence. The GOES launched the Recreational Schools Program, which benefitted 1,700 young people from 12 schools in San Vicente, La Paz, and Cuscatlan. The USG completed municipal violence diagnostics in 13 selected high-risk municipalities and provided assistance for the development of Municipal Prevention Plans and biannual action plans to reduce violence and youth involvement in gangs. A baseline study for each of the 13 municipalities to measure the impact of prevention interventions was completed. The USG is providing $5.8 million for the implementation of the plans. The municipalities will also contribute close to $500,000 each in additional funding for the activities. An institutional assessment of PREPAZ, the Ministry of Justice and Public Security's prevention unit, was completed. Additionally, 71 PREPAZ and 40 members of Municipal Violence Prevention Committees from 20 municipalities were trained in developing municipal violence diagnostics in accordance with the national strategy. Municipal Violence Prevention Committees in San Martin and Ciudad Arce developed annual operating plans and trained to 1,027 children and youth in life skills, conflict resolution, and leadership. An Investment Board was established to promote the role of the private sector in crime and violence prevention, and a partnership was initiated with Arizona State University to conduct research in the area of prevention.

Goal 12: Reduce overcrowding in prisons, thereby allowing the Salvadoran prison system to safely, securely, and humanely manage an increasing population.	Behind Schedule

Prison overcrowding continues at over 317 percent. The USG continues to provide equipment and training to assist the Prison Directorate (DGCP). However, more needs to be done to manage both personnel and resources more effectively. Two inmate transport vans and a 43-passenger inmate transport bus were donated to the DGCP, which will facilitate transportation of inmates who are part of YO CAMBIO, a program that allows inmates to trade work for reduced jail time. The number of participants in the YO CAMBIO program has increased by 300 percent since November 2013. Blueprints and procurement plans have been finalized to house those participating in the expansion of the YO CAMBIO dormitories in San Miguel, Santa Ana, and Usulután. The acquisition of the materials will begin in June 2014 to expand program capacity by 778 inmates. The GOES signed a loan agreement focused on strengthening the prison system, which includes over $71 million in financing from the Central American Bank for Economic Integration (BCIE) and a GOES counterpart of over $8 million. The loan would include construction of facilities, expansion of current prison farms, and electronic control systems such as ankle bracelets. However, regulations for the implementation of an electronic surveillance system still have not been approved.

Goal 13: Enhance the security of the prisons for their improvement as correctional facilities, prevent them from perpetuating and magnifying criminal activity in El Salvador, and help former offenders become full, contributing members of society.	Behind Schedule

Special Investigative Units (SIUs) have been equipped and are operational in 13 of the 19 prisons in the GOES penal system. However, information regarding reports generated by the SIUs needed to be shared more broadly. Nine pickup trucks as well as UFED CELLBRITE cell-phone chip readers, laptops, ballistic vests and riot gear were purchased and donated to the DGCP to improve general prison management. The donated equipment is valued at approximately $1 million. The USG also supported the purchase and installation of audio-video communication equipment in the Zacatecaluca Maximum Security Prison. Efforts to reinforce prison cells with cell-phone blockers for high-risk maximum security inmates have not had the desired effect and illicit activities continue to occur from within the prison system. Reforms to the Telecommunications Law were presented to the Legislative Assembly on December 12, 2013, the purpose of which is to ensure that phone signals around prisons do not exceed the capacity levels defined by the Superintendence of Electricity and Telecommunications (SIGET). Recent raids at prisons have recovered hundreds of cell phones, laptop computers, Bluetooth devices, chargers, batteries, weapons, drugs and other communication devices used by inmates. Turning that evidence over to the Attorney General to develop prosecutions is a critical next step. Materials and equipment were donated for the renovation of a job skills program in La Esperanza (Mariona) prison.

Goal 14: Promote the use of extraditions as a deterrent for crime and a means to reinforce national security.	On Track

On December 18, 2013, Salvadoran citizen Edgar Benitez was extradited to the United States. This represents only the second extradition of a Salvadoran citizen to the U.S. in more than 100 years. During this reporting period, the Supreme Court of El Salvador approved two extraditions and three requests for provisional arrest warrants. The USG has developed a draft standard flow procedure to help systemize the extradition process for both the USG and the GOES. However, for extradition to be an effective crime reduction tool in the long term, development of GOES procedures and strategies regarding the extradition process must be enhanced and further systematized. The appointment of a GOES Point of Contact for this Goal is anticipated in the coming months and will be vital to moving this goal forward.

CONSTRAINT 2: LOW PRODUCTIVITY IN THE TRADABLES SECTOR

Goal 1: Facilitate the establishment of a Growth Council to promote an environment of trust and improve the business climate and investments in activities or sectors regarded as strategic.	On Track

President-elect Sanchez Ceren invited the Growth Council's private sector members to remain for the new administration. The reforms to the Public-Private Partnership (PPP) law, which the Council and its technical team developed, were passed by the Legislative Assembly on April 25. A law establishing PROESA as a semi-autonomous institution and the primary

GOES entity responsible for managing PPP development was also passed in April. Other legislation, such as the Judicial Stability Law and the Electronic Signature Law, remain pending in the Legislative Assembly. The November 2013 forum on "Strategies for Strengthening the Value Chain of Shrimp and Synthetic Fiber" and the January 2014 forum "Challenges in Reactivating the Cacao Sector in El Salvador" were organized to enhance growth in strategic tradables sectors. The FUSADES private sector business climate perception survey continued to reveal a negative trend with a 48 percent unfavorable opinion in the most recent report (last three months of 2013), with only 10 percent perceiving a favorable climate. El Salvador's rank in the Doing Business Report remains as reported in the previous Scorecard, having decreased to 118 out of 189 countries in the 2013-2014 report from 113 out of 185 countries in the 2012-2013 report.

Goal 2: Reduce firms' costs due to infrastructure to improve their competitiveness.	On Track

The International Airport is scheduled to complete its $20 million runway overlay project in May. The remaining $50 million of airport rehabilitation projects are on time and budget. The U.S. Trade and Development Agency (USTDA)-funded Airport Master Plan was completed, which CEPA presented at an international air service conference in El Salvador in February. Delta Airlines announced new service to Los Angeles, and Southwest Airlines indicated interest in entering the market. Efforts continue to concession La Union Port; there are four pre-qualified bidders. The CEPA Board approved the tender and PPP documents for May issuance with contract award in late 2014. The GOES offered to fund dredging costs ($15-25 million annually) for the 30-year concession. CEPA continues to pay the associated JICA debt and will enter into a currency hedge (to minimize exchange rate exposure from the Yen-denominated debt). USTDA is providing a grant for a channel navigation aids study. CEPA is evaluating $8 million in self-funded improvements to the Acajutla port. In May, MCC financed IKONS (Chile) to perform a Value for Money study on the international airport expansion plan. Maryland Governor Martin O'Malley established an agreement with CEPA to support the airport modernization and expansion projects. The National Energy Council finished a new legal framework for renewable energy investments. A solicitation of 15 MW of small-scale renewable energy projects was recently awarded to 42 companies. Another solicitation for 100 MW of solar and wind energy projects is underway. The municipality of Santa Tecla accepted a pilot project proposal to install energy efficient street lighting. Investment in infrastructure as a percentage of GDP decreased slightly from the prior reporting period, from 6.12 percent to 6.07 percent. The Global Competitive Infrastructure Index remained unchanged with El Salvador ranked at 72.

Goal 3: Improve the quality of the education system in order to create a more highly qualified and technologically skilled labor force. The Governments of El Salvador and the United States will join forces to help ensure that education of the labor supply matches labor market demand.	On Track

The USG provided training to 239 English teachers and 200 students continuing English studies. Under a USAID program, 111 high school students graduated after receiving specialized courses in English and Information Technology, and 87 percent will pursue a college degree. Twenty students were given scholarships to study in community colleges in the U.S. The USG offered 13 seminars on science and technology at Don Bosco University. The GOES, through the Salvadoran Institute for Professional Training (INSAFORP), invited bids for the National English for Work Program, developed in conjunction with the USG, to teach English to 4,000 participants. INSAFORP, working with the USG, trained 53 youth in basic competencies for entry-level employment, resulting in 32 job placements. In addition, 400 youth were trained in information and communications technology (ICT), and INSAFORP trained 3,642 workers in ICT. INSAFORP, together with the private and academic sectors, produced a study on future professional training for occupations supporting tradables. As previously reported, the Global Competitiveness Index for 2013-14 ranked El Salvador 100 out of 148 countries in the "Higher Education and Training" sub-index; and 121 of 148 countries in the sub-index on "Labor Market Efficiency." Both showed a slight improvement in respect to the 2012-2013 sub-indexes.

Goal 4: Raise (net) tax revenues to 16 percent of GDP by 2015 and use public resources efficiently and transparently. These goals are also included in the implementation of the fiscal pact, which is an integral part of the PQD priority areas, as defined by the Economic and Social Cabinet.	On Track

The USG provided technical assistance to the Ministry of Finance (MOF) to improve taxpayer information and database systems. The assistance supporting the implementation of web services and five modules of the automated Case Selection Management System (CSMS) II tool is expected to reduce tax evasion. To improve the transparent and efficient use of public resources, Phase II of the new fiscal transparency portal was completed with trilateral assistance between the GOES, the USG, and the Government of Brazil. Experts from Brazil also provided technical assistance to the MOF upgrading the Fiscal Transparency Portal. The USG is assisting the GOES in improving its legal and accounting systems and to prepare a result-oriented budget process in several sectors. Other actions completed include the approval of the accounting conceptual model under International Public Sector Accounting Standards (IPSAS), the approval of the government chart of accounts under IPSAS, design of Phase I of the SAFI II budget implementation modules, and completion of the Phase I of the GOES online procurement portal COMPRASAL II. The percentage of net tax collected relative to GDP increased from 14.4 percent in the fourth quarter of 2012, to 15.3 percent in the fourth quarter of 2013. There was no update in El Salvador's score in the Open Budget Index and so remains at 43 out of 100 ranked countries.

Goal 5: Support a strategy for attracting and promoting FDI and making El Salvador a more attractive place for foreign investment. The measures described are aimed at streamlining the establishment of operations for potential investors and simultaneously focusing on scaling up efforts to promote and attract investments.	Behind Schedule

Legislation to strengthen the Salvadoran Export Promotion Agency (PROESA) was passed by the Legislative Assembly in April. This legislation establishes PROESA as a semi-autonomous institution with a mandate to promote and develop investment, exports, and public private partnerships (PPP). PROESA continues to build its internal capacity in preparation for overseeing PPP development, but a permanent Executive Director of PROESA was not named during this reporting period. With support from the Inter-American Development Bank (IDB), PROESA has begun the development of a country image strategy aimed at improving El Salvador's international reputation. The International Financial Corporation (IFC) has continued its work with the Growth Council on reforms to improve the business climate. As part of an effort to improve corporate governance, the IFC delivered a diagnostic report on reforms to strengthen minority stakeholders' rights. At the municipal level, IFC officially launched the subnational Doing Business in El Salvador project that will include San Salvador, Santa Ana, San Miguel, and Soyapango. Additionally, 40 of the 50 Municipal Competitiveness Committees assisted by the USG are engaging in public-private dialogues to improve the local business environment. Foreign direct investment as a percentage of GDP decreased to 0.6 percent in 2013 from 2.2 percent in 2012. On the Future Brand's Country Brand Index, El Salvador improved its position to 107 of 118 countries in 2012- 2013 from 109 of 113 countries in 2011-2012 (as reported in the previous Scorecard).

Goal 6: Surmount low productivity of tradables by transforming factors of production of the tradables sector through the implementation of strategies to improve innovation and quality, and a focus on the international market.	On Track

The Ministry of Economy's Productive Development Fund (FONDEPRO) granted $1.9 million in co-financing to 111 SMEs implementing 139 business initiatives that generated 620 jobs. The GOES approved an additional $6.4 million to strengthen institutions providing business development services to support SME export activities. The GOES and the private sector developed a work plan to promote six key economic sectors (aeronautics, textiles, chemical-pharmaceuticals, plastics, electronics, and distance business services) that offer comparative advantages. With USG support, the GOES and the private sector launched a new Small Business Development Center (SBDC), bringing the total of such centers to 12. The 1,969 businesses assisted by SBDCs in 2013 yielded domestic sales and exports of $11.3 million, a 143 percent increase, and generated 3,430 jobs. The USG provided international business development assistance to 483 businesses. These firms increased domestic sales and exports by $6.3 million, generating 760 jobs. A $255,000 grant was approved by the USG for the FUPEC Foundation to work with Salvadoran hometown associations in the U.S., extending assistance to microbusinesses and grassroots associations in El Salvador. El Salvador ranked 60 of 148 countries in Business Sophistication in the 2013-2014 Global Competitiveness Index, an improvement of 22 positions (as reported in the previous scorecard), while. The number of export companies with sales over $500,000 decreased to 474 firms for January-February 2014, from 542 in 2013.

In: El Salvador
Editor: Joelle Foster

ISBN: 978-1-63321-766-9
© 2014 Nova Science Publishers, Inc.

Chapter 3

EL SALVADOR 2013 HUMAN RIGHTS REPORT[*]

U.S. Department of State; Bureau of Democracy, Human Rights and Labor

EXECUTIVE SUMMARY

El Salvador is a constitutional multi-party republic. In 2009 voters elected Carlos Mauricio Funes Cartagena of the Farabundo Marti National Liberation Front (FMLN) as president for a five-year term in generally free and fair elections. Free and fair legislative assembly and municipal elections took place in March 2012. Authorities failed at times to maintain effective control over the security forces. Security forces committed human rights abuses.

The principal human rights problems were widespread corruption; weaknesses in the judiciary and the security forces that contributed to a high level of impunity; and abuse, including domestic violence, discrimination, and commercial sexual exploitation against women and children.

Other human rights problems included isolated unlawful killings and cruel treatment by security forces; lengthy pretrial detention; harsh and life-threatening prison conditions; some restrictions on freedom of speech and press; trafficking in persons; and discrimination against persons with

---

[*] This is an edited, reformatted and augmented version of a report released by the U.S. Department of State; Bureau of Democracy, Human Rights and Labor, updated March 21, 2014.

disabilities and persons with HIV/AIDS. There was also widespread discrimination and some violence against lesbian, gay, bisexual, and transgender (LGBT) persons. Child labor and inadequate enforcement of labor laws also were problems.

Impunity persisted despite the government taking steps to dismiss some officials who committed abuses in the penitentiary system and within the police force.

SECTION 1. RESPECT FOR THE INTEGRITY OF THE PERSON, INCLUDING FREEDOM FROM:

a. Arbitrary or Unlawful Deprivation of Life

During the year there were no verified reports that the government or its agents committed politically motivated killings; however, there were reports of security force involvement in unlawful killings. As of August, the Office of the Ombudsman for Human Rights (PDDH) received 15 complaints of alleged unlawful killings committed by security, military, and other public officials. Three of the killings took place in the prison system and one in a police detention center.

The PDDH has the authority to investigate (but not prosecute) human rights abuses and refers all human rights abuse cases to the Office of the Attorney General (FGR). Although the PDDH defines all killings by government personnel as "extrajudicial killings," there were no verifiable reports of deliberate, unlawful killings carried out by order of the government or with its complicity. As of June, the Office of the Inspector General (IG) of the National Civilian Police (PNC) reported that 14 PNC officers were accused of homicide during the year but did not specify whether the perpetrators committed the killings while on duty.

On March 2, the PNC detained two officers for the killing of prisoner Mario Alexander Reyes Chavez, who was being held in a police detention center in Los Planes de Renderos as a protected witness to a drug trafficking case. A PNC commissioner said Chavez was shot between 25 and 28 times. On March 7, nine of the 14 police officers who were working in the detention center were jailed and were awaiting trial. Reyes Chavez had alerted the PNC that he had received death threats. The media reported that prior to the killing, intelligence officials had notified PNC authorities three times about visits of strangers to the detention center and encouraged authorities to increase security, yet the PNC did not take action. On October 10, a judge absolved a gang member accused of being the mastermind of the murder.

b. Disappearance

There were no reports of politically motivated disappearances. The nongovernmental organization (NGO) Association for the Search for Missing Children (Pro-Busqueda) received seven new complaints regarding children who disappeared during the 1980-1992 civil war. As of July it continued to investigate 538 cases and resolved 14 other cases.

c. Torture and Other Cruel, Inhuman, or Degrading Treatment or Punishment

The law prohibits such practices. The PDDH, however, received 89 complaints of torture or cruel, inhumane, or degrading treatment or punishment perpetrated by public officials, involving 58 complaints against PNC officials and 13 against members of the armed forces. The PDDH also received 445 complaints about violations of human integrity, 324 against PNC officers and 44 against members of the armed forces. The PDDH received complaints of unauthorized searches, mistreatment, physical abuse, insults, and harassment committed by the military in their conduct of joint patrols with the PNC. The Ministry of Defense alleges it investigated all cases against members of the armed forces, but released no results of the investigations publicly.

On June 1, doctors reported that a severely beaten prisoner in Apanteos Prison died during a subsequent surgery. The victim's mother accused the prison guards of beating her son. The doctors in the hospital where he was being treated alerted the FGR of the case. The hospital reported he died of pneumonia, not as a result of his severe injuries.

NGOs reported that public officials, including police, engaged in violence and discrimination against sexual minorities. Persons from the LGBT community stated that the agencies in charge of processing identification documents, the PNC and FGR, harassed transgender and gay individuals when they applied for identification cards or reported cases of violence against LGBT persons. The LGBT community reported that authorities harassed

LGBT persons through strip searches and questioning their gender in a degrading manner. The government responded to these abuses primarily through PDDH reports that publicized specific cases of violence and discrimination against sexual minorities.

Prison and Detention Center Conditions

Prison and detention center conditions remained harsh and life threatening.

Physical Conditions

Overcrowding was a serious threat to prisoners' health and lives. In many facilities, provisions for sanitation, potable water, ventilation, temperature, medical care, and lighting were inadequate. As of September 3, the Prison Directorate reported 26,672 prisoners held in 23 correctional facilities and one secure hospital ward that had a combined appropriate capacity of 8,328. The prison population included 20,454 convicted prisoners and 6,218 inmates held in pretrial detention. As of September, there were 2,598 female prisoners. As of September, there were 701 inmates in four prisons for juvenile offenders with a total appropriate capacity of 460 inmates. According to the director general of the prison system, as of September prison overcrowding was at 320 percent. Due to prison overpopulation, police authorities held some pretrial detainees in small detention centers at police stations. As of August police authorities held over 3,000 detainees in police station detention centers with a combined appropriate capacity of 1,200. Approximately 78 percent of these pretrial detainees were in detention centers longer than the 72 hours permitted by law before a suspect must be presented to court.

Due to the lack of holding cells, authorities often held pretrial detainees in regular prisons with violent criminals. Men were separated from women within the prisons. A separate women's prison in Ilopango was generally clean and allowed inmates' children under age five to stay with their mothers.

As of September 3, prison authorities reported that 36 prisoners died during the year due to natural causes, homicide, and suicide.

Gang activities in prisons and juvenile-holding facilities remained a serious problem. Detention center facilities held 10,576 inmates who were current or former gang members. Officials separated gang members from the regular prison population when possible, but gangs continued to exercise influence within the prisons and judicial system.

Prisoners reportedly conducted criminal activities from their cells, at times with the complicity of prison guards. Smuggling of weapons, drugs, and other contraband such as cell phones and cell-phone SIM cards was a major problem in the prisons.

As of September 3, prison authorities removed three guards from prisons for carrying illegal objects and sanctioned 100 guards for misconduct. There were no reported patterns of abuse of persons with disabilities in prisons, although the government's National Council for Comprehensive Attention to Persons with Disability (CONAIPD) reported isolated incidents, including sexual abuse.

Administration

Prison authorities kept detailed electronic records of all prisoners. Authorities allowed release on bail for some nonviolent offenders. The Solicitor's Office implemented a mediation program, principally for cases related to family disputes. The Attorney General's Office and the courts also have mediation programs and other alternative dispute resolution programs. In certain misdemeanor cases related to damages, judges suspended the judicial process when the defendant admitted guilt and adequately compensated the victim. Although there is no prison ombudsman, the PDDH oversees the rights of inmates and responded to complaints. Prisoners and detainees had reasonable access to visitors and religious observance.

Prison authorities permitted prisoners and detainees to submit complaints to judicial authorities without censorship and to request investigation of credible allegations of inhumane conditions. Prison authorities investigated such allegations, although investigators did not always document results in a publicly accessible manner.

Independent Monitoring

The government investigated and monitored prison and detention center conditions and permitted prison-monitoring visits by independent human rights observers, NGOs, and the media.

Church groups, the Central American University's Human Rights Institute, and other groups visited prisons during the year.

d. Arbitrary Arrest or Detention

Although the constitution prohibits arbitrary arrest and detention, there were complaints that the PNC arbitrarily arrested and detained persons. The PDDH reported receiving 137complaints of illegal detentions.

Role of the Police and Security Apparatus

The PNC, overseen by the ministry of justice and public security, is responsible for maintaining public security and the ministry of defense for maintaining national security. The military is tasked with securing the international border and conducting patrols jointly with the PNC. Military personnel assigned to assist the PNC do not have arrest authority. President Funes renewed the decree authorizing military involvement in police duties through May 2014.

On May 17, the Supreme Court ruled unconstitutional the appointments of retired general Francisco Ramon Salinas Rivera as PNC director and retired general David Munguia Payes as Minister of Justice and Public Security due to their ties with the military. The constitution separates public security functions from the military.

Inadequate training, lack of enforcement of the administrative police career law, arbitrary promotions, insufficient government funding, failure to effectively enforce evidentiary rules, and instances of corruption and criminality limited the PNC's effectiveness. As of September 12, the IG reported that authorities charged 14 police officers with homicide. The IG also received 1,163 complaints of alleged police misconduct, referred 473 of these cases to the FGR, and sanctioned 1,006 officers in response to complaints filed during the year and in prior years. These sanctions included 121 officers dismissed for misconduct and 677 suspended without pay. As of August 28, the FGR investigated 217 accusations against police officers, resulting in 29 cases resolved through mediation and two convictions.

The IG reported that most PNC officers and police academy cadets received human rights awareness training during the year, including training by the Salvadoran Institute for the Development of Women (ISDEMU), the Human Rights Institute of the University of Central America, and the Inter-American Institute of Human Rights. The PNC reported that as of July, 2,728 police officers received training on human rights.

Arrest Procedures and Treatment While in Detention

The constitution requires a written warrant for arrest, except in cases where an individual is arrested in the act of committing a crime. Authorities apprehended persons with warrants based on evidence and issued by a duly authorized official. The constitution grants detainees the right to a prompt judicial determination of the legality of their detention, and authorities generally respected this right. Police generally informed detainees promptly of charges against them.

The law permits release on bail for detainees who are unlikely to flee or whose release would not impede the investigation of the case. The bail system functioned adequately in most cases. The courts generally enforced a ruling that interrogation without the presence of counsel is coercive and that evidence obtained in such a manner is inadmissible. As a result PNC authorities generally delayed questioning until a public defender or an attorney arrived. Family members are allowed prompt access to detainees. Detainees generally had prompt access to counsel of their choice or to an attorney provided by the state.

The constitution permits the PNC to hold a person for 72 hours before presenting the suspect to court, after which the judge may order detention for an additional 72 hours to determine if an investigation is warranted. The law allows up to six months for investigation of serious crimes before requiring either a trial or dismissal of the case. In exceptionally complicated cases, the prosecutor may ask an appeals court to extend the deadline for three or six months, depending on the seriousness of the crime. Many cases were not completed within the legally prescribed period. In March the UN Working Group on Arbitrary Detention issued a report indicating that at the time of their 2012 visit to El Salvador, 7,376 detainees were in preventive detention, 937 of whom had exceeded the maximum one-year period of preventive detention allowed by law before sentencing must occur.

Arbitrary Arrest

The PDDH reported 137 complaints of arbitrary detention.

Pretrial Detention

Lengthy pretrial detention was a significant problem. At year's end, 24 percent of the prison population was in pretrial detention. Lengthy legal procedures, large numbers of detainees, judicial inefficiency, corruption, and staff shortages caused trial delays. Because it may take several years for a case to come to trial, some detainees were incarcerated longer than the maximum legal sentences for their alleged crimes. In such circumstances, detainees could request a Supreme Court review of their continued detention.

e. Denial of Fair Public Trial

Although the constitution provides for an independent judiciary, the judiciary suffered from inefficiency, corruption, political infighting, and insufficient resources. Substantial corruption in the judicial system contributed to a high level of impunity, undermining the rule of law and the public's respect for the judiciary. The criminal conviction rate was less than 5 percent. An ineffective public security strategy, inadequate government funding and training of the PNC, and ineffective senior-level leadership made it difficult to identify, arrest, and prosecute perpetrators of human rights abuses and other crimes, thus diminishing public confidence in the justice system. Intimidation and killing of police officers, crime victims, and witnesses created a climate of fear, complicating investigation of violent crime and other alleged human rights abuses.

The Legislative Assembly did not always comply with Supreme Court rulings. On January 24, the Supreme Court Constitutional Chamber ruled that the nominations of three individuals by the Legislative Assembly to the Court of Accounts were unconstitutional due to political party affiliation. On March 20, the Legislative Assembly disregarded this ruling by re-nominating two of these individuals and a replacement. The Supreme Court again ruled the nominations unconstitutional. On July 25, the Legislative Assembly finally nominated three new individuals not subsequently challenged.

On June 20, a UN special rapporteur issued a report criticizing the Legislative Assembly for not complying with the Supreme Court's rulings during the 2012 constitutional crisis.

As of July, the PNC was providing protection to 52 victims and 89 witnesses. However, some judges denied anonymity to witnesses at trial, and gang intimidation and violence against witnesses contributed to a climate of impunity from criminal prosecution.

During the year, the FGR received three complaints against judges, and the Supreme Court dismissed two judges as of June. During the year the FGR investigated one complaint against a prosecutor for misconduct. No convictions were reported as of October.

Trial Procedures

Although juries were used for specific charges, including environmental pollution and certain misdemeanors, judges decided most cases. By law, juries hear only cases that the law does not assign to sentencing courts. After the jury's determination of innocence or guilt, a tribunal decides the sentence.

Defendants have the right to be present in court, question witnesses, and present witnesses and evidence. The constitution further provides for the presumption of innocence, the right to be informed promptly and in detail of charges, the right to a fair and public trial without undue delay, the right to a trial by jury, protection from self-incrimination, the right to communicate with an attorney of choice, the right to adequate time and facilities to prepare a defense, freedom from coercion, the right to confront adverse witnesses and present one's own witnesses and evidence, the right to appeal, access for defendants and their attorneys to government-held evidence relevant to their cases, and government-provided legal counsel for the indigent. These legal rights and protections, however, were not always respected. Although a jury's verdict is final, a judge's verdict can be appealed. Trials are public. The law extends these rights to all citizens.

Political Prisoners and Detainees
There were no reports of political prisoners or detainees.

Civil Judicial Procedures and Remedies
The law provides for access to the courts, enabling litigants to bring civil lawsuits seeking damages for, as well as cessation of, human rights violations. Domestic court orders generally were enforced.

Regional Human Rights Court Decisions
Individuals or organizations may submit petitions for cases involving violations of an individual's human rights to the Inter-American Commission on Human Rights, which in turn may submit the case to the Inter-American Court of Human Rights. The court can order civil remedies including fair compensation to the individual injured. On May 29, in response to a petition filed by the Inter-American Commission on Human Rights on behalf of a woman pregnant with a non-viable fetus whose doctors diagnosed as at risk of dying due to pregnancy complications from preexisting conditions, the Inter-American Court of Human Rights ordered the government to adopt necessary measures to protect the woman's health. On June 4, the Health Ministry allowed a premature caesarian section and reported the baby died five hours after the procedure.

f. Arbitrary Interference with Privacy, Family, Home, or Correspondence

The constitution prohibits such actions, and the government generally respected these prohibitions in practice.

SECTION 2. RESPECT FOR CIVIL LIBERTIES, INCLUDING:

a. Freedom of Speech and Press

The constitution provides for freedom of speech and press, and the government generally respected these rights in practice. However, some restrictions on the freedom of speech and press occurred throughout the year. The law permits the executive branch to use the emergency broadcasting service to take over all broadcast and cable networks temporarily to televise political programming. The president occasionally used this law to highlight his accomplishments.

Freedom of Speech
Individuals could criticize the government publicly or privately without reprisal, and in most cases the government did not interfere with such criticism. On June 26, the Legislative Assembly issued a decree prohibiting individuals from expressing opinions that would defame presidential candidates. Responding to pressure from civil society, President Funes vetoed this decree on July 16.

Press Freedoms
The independent media were active and expressed a wide variety of views with some restrictions. There was no significant restriction by the government to the publication of books. On October 23, the Supreme Electoral Tribunal (TSE) determined that media companies had disseminated three political television advertisements that constituted "dirty campaigning," and established sanctions for those media companies. There is no legal provision for the TSE to sanction media companies. The media companies complained the ruling was discriminatory and a violation of freedom of speech.

Violence and Harassment
On June 4, construction workers in San Miguel threatened channel 12 reporter Angel Lemus, forcibly took his camera, and physically prevented him from leaving his car for 20 minutes. Lemus and Geovanny Giron were filming construction machinery belonging to the San Miguel municipality being used at the private residence of the San Miguel mayor. The PNC arrested 14 construction workers following the incident. The case was under investigation.

Censorship or Content Restrictions

Government advertising accounted for a significant portion of press advertising income, although exact data was not publicly available. Newspaper editors and radio directors occasionally discouraged journalists from reporting on topics that the owners or publishers might not view favorably. According to the Salvadoran Association of Journalists (APES), the media practiced self-censorship, especially in its reporting on gangs and narcotics trafficking. APES stated that many members of the media were afraid to report in detail on these subjects due to fear of retaliation from gangs and narcotics trafficking groups.

Nongovernmental Impact

APES noted that journalists reporting on gangs and narcotics trafficking were subject to threats and intimidation, which led to media self-censorship.

Internet Freedom

There were no government restrictions on access to the internet or credible reports that the government monitored e-mail or internet chat rooms without appropriate legal authority. Individuals and groups could engage in the expression of views via the internet, including by e-mail. Internet access was available in public places throughout the country. The International Telecommunication Union reported that 25.5 percent of Salvadorans used the internet in 2012.

Academic Freedom and Cultural Events

There were no government restrictions on academic freedom or cultural events.

b. Freedom of Peaceful Assembly and Association

The constitution provides for freedom of assembly and association, and the government generally respected these rights in practice.

c. Freedom of Religion

See the Department of State's *International Religious Freedom Report* at www.state.gov/j/drl/irf/rpt/.

d. Freedom of Movement, Internally Displaced Persons, Protection of Refugees, and Stateless Persons

The constitution provides for freedom of internal movement, foreign travel, emigration, and repatriation; the government generally respected these rights in practice. The government cooperated with the Office of the UN High Commissioner for Refugees (UNHCR) and other humanitarian organizations in providing protection and assistance to internally displaced persons, refugees, returning refugees, asylum seekers, stateless persons, and other persons of concern.

Protection of Refugees

Access to Asylum
The law provides for the granting of asylum or refugee status, and the government has established a system for providing protection to refugees. As of September 11, the government received two refugee petitions and had not made a decision on the petitions.

SECTION 3. RESPECT FOR POLITICAL RIGHTS: THE RIGHT OF CITIZENS TO CHANGE THEIR GOVERNMENT

The constitution provides citizens the right to change their government peacefully, and citizens exercised this right in practice through periodic, free, and fair elections based on universal suffrage.

Elections and Political Participation

Recent Elections
Legislative Assembly elections were held in March 2012, and independent observer groups reported the elections were free and fair with few irregularities. During these elections as in prior elections, the ARENA and FMLN political parties accused each other of registering noncitizen voters

from other countries under the registration law, which allows a person to register with two witnesses who swear to his/her identity.

Participation of Women and Minorities

There were 23 women in the 84-member Legislative Assembly, six women on the 15-member Supreme Court, and three women in the 13-member cabinet. No members of the Supreme Court, the legislature, or other government entities identified themselves as members of an ethnic minority or indigenous community, and there were no political party positions or parliamentary seats designated for ethnic minorities.

SECTION 4. CORRUPTION AND LACK OF TRANSPARENCY IN GOVERNMENT

The law provides criminal penalties for corruption by officials; however, the government did not implement the law effectively, and officials often engaged in corrupt practices with impunity. The NGO Institute for Social Democracy stated that officials, particularly in the judicial system, often engaged in corrupt practices with impunity.

Corruption

There are five offices that share responsibility for combating corruption: the Court of Accounts, a chamber of the Supreme Court that acts as a transparency office and an accountability court; the Sub-Secretariat for Transparency and Anticorruption, an Executive Branch agency that implements the e-government initiative and heads official newspapers; the Anticorruption Unit of the FGR, which leads crime investigations regarding corruption; the Supreme Court Probity Section, which enforces the illicit enrichment law; and the Government Ethics Tribunal, an Administrative Court that sanctions those public officers who commit irregularities in their duties.

NGOs, including the Salvadoran Foundation for Economic and Social Development (FUSADES), alleged that the Supreme Court did not adequately deal with corrupt judges and that perceived corruption and weak application of criminal law by judges contributed to a lack of confidence in the judiciary. As of June 30, according to FUSADES, the Supreme Court had not resolved over 1,000 complaints against justices. As of June 30, the Supreme Court resolved 28 cases against judges, resulting in the dismissal of two judges, the suspension of 16 judges, and the dismissal of charges for 10 judges. FUSADES maintained a website that makes judicial proceedings and records available to the public.

As of September 13, the Ethics Tribunal received 166 complaints involving 407 public officers. The tribunal resolved 189 complaints from its multi-year caseload, imposed six sanctions, and submitted five cases to the FGR.

On March 4, the media reported that the Legislative Assembly had spent $150,000 (the U.S. dollar is the national currency of El Salvador) on artwork during 2012, which represented more than double the amount of money that had been spent on artwork over the previous 15 years combined. Media also reported that some of the artwork had disappeared from the Legislative Assembly.

Civil society groups strongly criticized the Legislative Assembly for this expense, especially in light of the significant budget constraints facing the government.

Whistleblower Protection

The law does not provide protection to public and private employees for making internal disclosures or lawful public disclosures of evidence of illegality.

Financial Disclosure

The Illicit Enrichment Law requires appointed and elected officials to submit their assets records to the Probity Section of the Supreme Court. The declarations are not made available to the public, and the law does not establish sanctions for noncompliance.

Public Access to Information

The law provides for the right of access to government information. Although the law established mechanisms to appeal denials of information, the authorities did not effectively implement the law. The law provides a narrow list of exceptions outlining the grounds for nondisclosure, a reasonably short timeline for the relevant authority to disclose or respond, no processing fees, and administrative sanctions for noncompliance.

Some public officers refused to publish information. For example, as of October 31, Legislative Assembly President Sigfrido Reyes had refused to reveal the salaries of legislative assembly advisors, even after the Access to Information Institute twice ordered him to do so.

On February 8, the Legislative Assembly passed amendments that significantly weakened the Public Information Access Law by expanding the amount of government information that could be withheld from public disclosure and reducing civil society's power to nominate the commissioners of the Access to Information Institute, the entity responsible for enforcing the law. Responding to pressure from civil society, President Funes vetoed the amendments on February 14, and on February 23 named the five commissioners, ending a nearly year-long delay in the nomination process.

SECTION 5. GOVERNMENTAL ATTITUDE REGARDING INTERNATIONAL AND NONGOVERNMENTAL INVESTIGATION OF ALLEGED VIOLATIONS OF HUMAN RIGHTS

A variety of domestic and international human rights groups generally operated without government restriction, investigating and publishing their findings on human rights cases. Although government officials generally were cooperative and responsive to these groups, officials at times were reluctant to discuss worker rights problems with NGOs and the PDDH. The government required domestic and international NGOs to register with the government, and some domestic NGOs reported that the government made the registration process unnecessarily difficult.

Government Human Rights Bodies

The principal human rights investigative and monitoring body is the autonomous PDDH, whose head the Legislative Assembly nominates to a three-year term. The PDDH regularly issued reports and press releases on prominent human rights cases. The PDDH generally enjoyed government cooperation, operated without government or party interference, had adequate resources, and was considered generally effective.

The PDDH maintained a constructive dialogue with the president's office. The government publicly acknowledged receipt of PDDH reports, although in some cases it did not take action on PDDH recommendations, which are non-binding.

SECTION 6. DISCRIMINATION, SOCIETAL ABUSES, AND TRAFFICKING IN PERSONS

Although the constitution and other laws provide that all persons are equal before the law and prohibit discrimination based on race, gender, disability, language, sexual orientation, gender identity, or social status, the government did not effectively enforce these prohibitions. There was discrimination against women, persons with disabilities, LGBT persons, and indigenous people. The Secretariat of Social Inclusion (SIS), headed by First Lady Vanda Pignato, made efforts to overcome traditional bias in all these areas.

Women

Rape and Domestic Violence
The law criminalizes rape, and the criminal code's definition of rape may apply to spousal rape. The law requires the FGR to prosecute rape cases whether or not the victim presses charges, and the law does not permit the victim to nullify the criminal charge. Generally, the penalty for rape is six to 10 years of imprisonment, but the law provides for a maximum sentence of 20 years for rape of certain classes of victims, including children and persons with disabilities.

Incidents of rape continued to be underreported for several reasons, including societal and cultural pressures on victims, fear of reprisal, ineffective and unsupportive responses by authorities toward victims, fear of publicity, and a perception among victims that cases were unlikely to be prosecuted. Laws against rape were not effectively enforced.

Rape and other sexual crimes against women were widespread. As of August 28, the FGR reported 4,826 cases of alleged sexual crimes resulting in

392 convictions during the year. As of October 10, the ISDEMU reported 3,466 cases of alleged sexual abuse, physical abuse, rape, and psychological abuse.

As of October, the ISDEMU provided health and psychological assistance to 5,535 women who experienced sexual abuse, domestic violence, mistreatment, sexual harassment, labor harassment, commercial sexual exploitation, trafficking in persons, or alien smuggling.

The law prohibits domestic violence and generally provides for sentences ranging from one to three years in prison, although some forms of domestic violence carry higher penalties. The law also permits obtaining restraining orders against offenders. Laws against domestic violence were not well enforced, and cases were not effectively prosecuted. A 2011 law prohibits mediation in domestic violence disputes.

Violence against women, including domestic violence, was a widespread and serious problem. As of July, the PNC reported 1,904 cases of alleged domestic violence. A large portion of the population considered domestic violence socially acceptable, and, as with rape, its incidence was underreported.

In June, in two separate incidents, two men set fire to their girlfriends following domestic disputes. Both women survived with injuries, and police arrested the two men. The cases were under investigation.

During the year President Funes engaged in a government campaign to support SIS in its efforts to eliminate violence against women. ISDEMU coordinated with the judicial and executive branches and civil society groups to conduct public awareness campaigns against domestic violence and sexual abuse. The PDDH, FGR, Supreme Court, Public Defender's Office, and PNC collaborated with NGOs and other organizations to combat violence against women through education, increased enforcement of the law, and NGO support for programs for victims. SIS, through ISDEMU, defined policies, programs, and projects on domestic violence and continued to maintain one shared telephone hotline and two separate shelters for victims of domestic abuse and child victims of commercial sexual exploitation. The government's efforts to combat domestic violence were minimally effective.

Sexual Harassment

The law prohibits sexual harassment and provides penalties of imprisonment from three to five years if the victim is an adult and from four to eight years if the victim is a minor. Fines can also be imposed, and additional fines are added to the prison term in cases where the perpetrator is in a position of authority or trust over the victim. The law also mandates that employers take measures to avoid sexual harassment, violence against women, and other workplace harassment problems. The law requires employers to create and implement preventative programs that address violence against women, sexual abuse, and other psychosocial risks. The government, however, did not enforce sexual harassment laws effectively.

Since underreporting by victims of sexual harassment appeared to be widespread, it was difficult to estimate the extent of the problem. As of August 28, the FGR reported 552 cases of alleged sexual harassment during the year, of which 33 resulted in convictions.

Reproductive Rights

Couples and individuals had the right to decide the number, spacing, and timing of children. Information about and access to contraception was widely available. Demographic Health Surveys indicated that 72 percent of married women used some method of family planning. Prenatal care and skilled attendance at delivery generally were available.

Discrimination

The constitution grants women and men the same legal rights under family and property law, but women did not enjoy equal treatment in practice. The law establishes sentences of one to three years in prison for public officials who deny a person's civil rights based on gender, and six months to two years for employers who discriminate against women in the workplace, but employees generally did not report such violations due to fear of employer reprisals.

Although pregnancy testing as a condition for employment is illegal, some businesses allegedly required female job applicants to present pregnancy test results, and some businesses illegally fired pregnant workers. As of October, the Ministry of Labor received 16 complaints regarding illegal firing of pregnant workers but imposed no fines.

Although the law prohibits discrimination based on gender, women suffered from cultural, economic, and societal discrimination. Although the law requires equal pay for equal work, the average wage paid to women for comparable work was 57 percent of that paid to men. Men often received priority in job placement and promotions, and women were not accorded equal treatment in traditional male-dominated sectors, such as agriculture and business. Training for women generally was confined to low- and middle-wage occupational areas where women already held most positions, such as teaching, nursing, apparel assembly, home industry, and small business.

Children

Birth Registration

Citizenship is derived by birth within the country and from one's parents. The law requires parents to register a child within 15 days of birth or pay a $2.86 fine. While firm statistics were unavailable, many births were not registered. Failure to register resulted in denial of school enrollment.

Education

Education is free, universal, and compulsory through the ninth grade and nominally free through high school. Rural areas frequently fell short of providing required education to all eligible students, due to a lack of resources and because rural parents often withdrew their children from school by the sixth grade to allow them to work.

Child Abuse

Child abuse was a serious and widespread problem. Incidents of rape continued to be underreported for a number of reasons, including societal and cultural pressures on victims, fear of reprisal against victims, ineffective and unsupportive responses by authorities toward victims, fear of publicity, and a perception among victims that cases were unlikely to be prosecuted.

The Salvadoran Institute for Children and Adolescents (ISNA), an autonomous government entity, defined policies, programs, and projects on child abuse; maintained a shelter for child victims of abuse and commercial sexual exploitation; and conducted a violence awareness campaign to combat child abuse. From January through September, ISNA reported sheltering 496 abused children in 11 shelters. According to a 2012 World Bank report, 41 percent of the first pregnancies of girls between the ages of 10 and 19 resulted from sexual abuse, and 12 percent of such pregnancies resulted from sexual abuse committed by a family member.

Forced and Early Marriage

The legal minimum age for marriage is 18, although the law authorizes marriage from the age of 14 if both the boy and girl have reached puberty, if the girl is pregnant or the couple has had a child. According to UNICEF, 5 percent of children were married by age 15 and 25 percent by age 18. UNFPA reported that the country lacked data disaggregated by demographic, social, and economic characteristics and therefore was unable to develop appropriate policies and programs to address forced and early marriage.

Sexual Exploitation of Children

Sexual exploitation of children remained a problem, and some girls were forced into prostitution. Child sex trafficking is covered under the trafficking-in-persons statutes in the penal code, which prescribe penalties of four to eight years' imprisonment for trafficking crimes. An offense committed against a child is considered an aggravated circumstance, and the penalty increases by one-third, but the government did not effectively enforce these laws.

The minimum age of consensual sex is 18. The law classifies statutory rape as sexual relations with anyone under age 18 and includes penalties between four and 20 years' imprisonment upon conviction. As of August 28, the FGR reported 1,445 cases of alleged rape of minors, resulting in 37 convictions.

The law prohibits paying anyone under the age of 18 for sexual services. As of December the ISNA trafficking-in-persons shelter, which admits only girls, had 11 girls who were victims of commercial sexual exploitation in residence. SIS, through ISDEMU, continued to maintain one shared telephone hotline for child victims of commercial sexual exploitation and victims of domestic abuse. The law prohibits participating in, facilitating, or purchasing materials containing child pornography and provides for prison sentences of up to 16 years.

International Child Abductions

The country is a party to the 1980 Hague Convention on the Civil Aspects of International Child Abduction. For information see the Department of State's annual report on compliance at www.travel.state. gov/abduction /resources/congressreport/congressreport_4308.h tml, as well as country-specific information at http://www.travel.state.gov/abduction/country /country 5819.html.

Anti-Semitism

There were no reports of anti-Semitic acts. The Jewish community totaled approximately 150 persons.

Trafficking in Persons

See the Department of State's *Trafficking in Persons Report* at www.state.gov/j/tip.

Persons with Disabilities

The law prohibits discrimination against persons with physical, sensory, intellectual, and mental disabilities in employment, education, air travel and other transportation, access to health care, or the provision of other state services. According to the government's National Council for Comprehensive Attention to Persons with Disability (CONAIPD), the government did not allocate sufficient resources to enforce these prohibitions effectively, particularly in education, employment, and transportation. The government did not effectively enforce legal requirements for access to buildings, information, and communications for persons with disabilities. There were almost no access ramps or provisions for the mobility of persons with disabilities. In general, children with disabilities attended school; however, at higher levels attendance was more dependent on their parents' financial resources.

CONAIPD, composed of representatives of multiple government entities, is the government agency responsible for protecting disability rights, but it lacks enforcement power.

Only 5 percent of businesses and no government agency fulfilled the legal requirement of hiring one person with disabilities for every 25 hires.

There were no reported patterns of abuse in educational or mental health facilities, although CONAIPD reported isolated incidents, including sexual abuse, in those facilities.

CONAIPD reported that persons frequently were fired after becoming disabled, persons with disabilities were not considered for work for which they qualified, and some schools would not accept children with disabilities due to lack of facilities and resources. There is no formal system for filing a complaint with the government.

During the year the SIS and CONAIPD conducted awareness campaigns, provided sensitivity training, promoted employment of persons with disabilities, and trained doctors and teachers about rights of persons with disabilities.

On June 19, the SIS secretary announced the launch of an education inclusion policy, a joint initiative of the SIS and the University of El Salvador that aims to eliminate discrimination against disabled persons in the academic and labor sectors.

Several public and private organizations promoted the rights of persons with disabilities, including the Telethon Foundation for Disabled Rehabilitation and the National Institute for Comprehensive Rehabilitation (ISRI). The Rehabilitation Foundation, in cooperation with ISRI, continued to operate a treatment center for persons with disabilities. However, CONAIPD reported that the government provided minimal funding for ISRI.

Indigenous People

In April 2012 the Legislative Assembly passed a constitutional reform recognizing the existence and the rights of indigenous peoples. The constitution states that native languages are part of the national heritage and should be preserved and respected. Births of indigenous persons were less likely to be registered officially, reducing educational opportunities, since school registration requires a birth certificate.

Although few individuals publicly identified themselves as indigenous, members of a few small indigenous communities continued to maintain traditional customs without repression or interference by the government or nonindigenous groups. Government estimates in 2004, the most recent available, indicated that approximately 99 percent of indigenous persons lived below the poverty level.

No laws provide indigenous people rights to share in revenue from exploitation of natural resources on indigenous lands. The government did not demarcate any lands as belonging to indigenous communities. Because few possessed title to land, opportunities for bank loans and other forms of credit were extremely limited. The PDDH reported that indigenous persons faced employment and workplace discrimination.

James Anaya, the UN special rapporteur on the rights of indigenous peoples, issued a final report on June 25 based on his 2012 visit. The report noted the effects of past violations of human rights created a situation where indigenous persons experienced widespread disadvantages. Anaya stated that indigenous people continued to suffer the loss of cultural knowledge and the capacity to demonstrate fully their identity and exercise the corresponding rights. He acknowledged the government's recent steps to recognize the existence of indigenous people and promote their human rights.

Societal Abuses, Discrimination, and Acts of Violence Based on Sexual Orientation and Gender Identity

Although the law prohibits discrimination on the basis of sexual orientation, discrimination was widespread. Transgender persons also experienced significant discrimination.

Widespread official and societal discrimination based on sexual orientation occurred in employment and access to health care and identity documents. NGOs reported that public officials, including police, engaged in violence and discrimination against sexual minorities. Persons from the LGBT community stated that the agencies in charge of processing identification documents, the PNC and FGR, ridiculed them when they applied for identification cards or reported cases of violence against LGBT persons. The government responded to these abuses primarily through PDDH reports that publicized specific cases of violence and discrimination against sexual minorities.

As of September 20, the PDDH investigated nine cases of possible human rights violations committed against LGBT persons, two of which involved abuses committed by the PNC and two others by municipal police. The PDDH received two reports of killings of transgender persons that had occurred in prior years.

On April 22, the UN Development Programme (UNDP) and the PDDH published a report on transgender women in El Salvador, stating that transgender women experienced violations of basic rights including access to education, employment, health care, and justice. Based on interviews with 100 transgender women cited in the UNDP study, only 36 percent received their high school degrees, and they reported facing harassment, violence, and exclusion in schools. Only 23.9 percent of the transgender women who suffered violence reported it to the authorities, and only one of the accused perpetrators was sanctioned.

As of September 11, human rights NGO Comcavis Trans reported that four transgender women and one gay man had been killed during the year. On May 5, the media reported the killing of Tania Vasquez, a transgender woman who was an employee of Comcavis Trans. Her body was found in a plastic bag and she died from a bullet. Comcavis Trans denounced the killing and urged the authorities to investigate the case. However, as of September 12, there were no updates on the case.

On May 16, the SIS Secretary launched a call center assistance hotline for the LGBT community designed to provide advice to the community on their rights and assistance to those suffering discrimination.

Other Societal Violence or Discrimination

Although the law prohibits discrimination on the basis of HIV/AIDS status, discrimination was widespread. Lack of public information and medical resources, fear of reprisal, fear of ostracism, and mild penalties incommensurate with the seriousness of the discrimination all remained problems in confronting discrimination against persons with HIV/AIDS or in assisting persons suffering from HIV/AIDS.

In January, the Atlacatl Association, an NGO that promotes the rights of persons with HIV/AIDS, publicly criticized several government agencies for failing to hire three individuals with HIV/AIDS and erroneously basing their decision on a 1961 Civil Service Law that prohibits hiring people with infectious or contagious illnesses. Atlacatl noted that in 2001, El Salvador passed a HIV/AIDS law that protects persons with HIV/AIDS from discrimination in employment. According to Atlacatl, in many instances employers provided a false reason for firing an employee with HIV/AIDS.

SECTION 7. WORKER RIGHTS

a. Freedom of Association and the Right to Collective Bargaining

The law provides for the right of most workers to form and join unions, to strike, to bargain collectively, and prohibits antiunion discrimination. The law, however, places several restrictions on these rights. Military personnel, national police, judges, high-level public officers, and workers who are in "positions of trust" are not permitted to form and join unions. The labor code does not cover public sector workers and municipal workers, who are regulated by the Civil Service Law.

Unions must meet complex requirements to legally register and have the right to bargain collectively, including a minimum membership of 35 workers. If the Ministry of Labor denies a union's legal registration, the law prohibits any attempt by the union to organize for the next six months. Collective bargaining is only obligatory if the union represents the majority of workers.

The law does not recognize the right to strike for public and municipal employees. Conflicts involving workers in essential services, which include those services where disruption would jeopardize or endanger life, security, health, or normal conditions of existence for some or all of the population. The law does not specify which services meet this definition. The law places several other restrictions on the right to strike, including the requirement that 30 percent of all workers in an enterprise must support a strike for it to be legal, and 51 percent must support the strike before all workers are bound by the decision to strike. In addition, unions may strike only to obtain or modify a collective bargaining agreement or to protect professional rights. They must also engage in negotiation, mediation, and arbitration processes before striking, though many groups often skip or go through these steps quickly. The law prohibits workers from appealing a government decision declaring a strike illegal.

The law does not require employers to reinstate illegally dismissed workers; instead, the law requires employers to pay illegally dismissed workers the equivalent of their basic salary for 30 days for each year of service completed, and this compensation must never be less than 15 days of basic salary. The law specifies 18 reasons for which an employer can legally suspend workers, and employers can invoke 11 of these reasons without prior administrative or judicial authorization.

The government did not effectively enforce the laws on freedom of association and the right to collective bargaining in all cases, and remedies and penalties remained ineffective. Judicial procedures were subject to lengthy delays and appeals. According to union representatives, the government did not consistently enforce labor rights for public workers, maquila/textile workers, subcontracted workers in the construction industry, security guards, informal sector workers, and migrant workers.

As of October 18, the Ministry of Labor received 47 complaints of violations of freedom of association, and imposed 1,614 fines totaling $397,152.35. The ministry also received 74 complaints of antiunion discrimination, and imposed 99 fines totaling $298,705.80. The ministry participated in mediation efforts for 16 complaints of illegal firings. Although not required by law, the Ministry of Labor continued to request some employers to rehire fired workers during the year, basing its requests on International Labor Organization (ILO) Administrative Court rulings. The ministry did not perform inspections in the informal sector. The ministry does not have jurisdiction over public employees, most of whom are governed by the Civil Service Law. Some long-term public employees not covered by the Civil Service Law were employed under temporary contracts despite being employed for as long as 10 years, allowing the government to dismiss these employees without paying severance.

In practice, workers faced challenges in exercising their rights to freedom of association and collective bargaining, including allegations by some unions of government influence on union activities and antiunion discrimination on the part of employers. Unions were independent of the government and political parties, although many generally were aligned with the ARENA, FMLN, or other political parties.

There were reports of antiunion discrimination, including threats against labor union members, dismissals of workers attempting to unionize, and blacklisting. Workers engaged in strikes regardless of whether legal requirements were met.

b. Prohibition of Forced or Compulsory Labor

The law prohibits all forms of forced or compulsory labor. The government generally did not effectively enforce such laws.

There were reports that some men and women were subjected to forced labor in agriculture, domestic servitude, and the informal sector. Some children were subjected to forced labor (see section 7.c.).

Also see the Department of State's *Trafficking in Persons Report* at www.state.gov/j/tip.

c. Prohibition of Child Labor and Minimum Age for Employment

The law prohibits the employment of children under age 14. The law allows children between the ages of 14 and 18 to engage in light work if the work does not damage the child's health or development, and cannot interfere with compulsory education. Children under age 16 are prohibited from working more than six hours per day and 34 hours per week; those under age 18 are prohibited from working at night or in occupations considered hazardous. The Ministry of Labor maintains a list of the types of work considered hazardous and prohibited for children, which include repairing heavy machinery; mining; handling weapons; fishing and harvesting mollusks; and working at heights above five feet while doing construction, erecting antennas, and working on billboards. Children age 16 and older are allowed to engage in light work on coffee and sugar plantations and in the fishing industry, so long as it does not harm their health or interfere with their education.

The Ministry of Labor is responsible for enforcing child labor laws but did so with limited effectiveness. The ministry's labor inspectors focused almost exclusively on the formal sector. As of October 18, the ministry reported that it encountered nine minors working without work permits, and 74 minors working with a special work permit. As of October 18, the government removed 14 boys from agricultural activities during the year. There was no information on any investigations or prosecutions by the government. The ministry lacked adequate resources to enforce effectively child labor laws in the agricultural sector, especially in coffee and sugarcane production and in the large informal sector.

During the year the Ministry of Labor conducted 12 campaigns to raise awareness about child labor. The government continued to participate in an ILO project to provide educational opportunities to children while offering livelihood alternatives for their families. The Ministry of Education promoted child labor awareness and encouraged school attendance, including operating after-school programs in 2,000 schools during the year. The Ministry of Governance and the Ministry of Agriculture also conducted awareness campaigns on child labor. The government also continued to include material on combating child labor in its elementary school curriculum.

Child labor remained a serious and widespread problem. The Ministry of Education reported that during the year the government identified 35,531 minors working in the agriculture sector, 1,450 minors working in the commerce and service industries, and 9,034 in domestic service. According to the 2011 School Registration Census, the most recent available, there were approximately 83,862 child workers, with the largest number engaged in agricultural work. The worst forms of child labor occurred in coffee and sugarcane cultivation, fishing, mollusk shucking, and fireworks production. There were reports of children engaged in garbage scavenging. Orphans and children from poor families frequently worked for survival as street vendors and general laborers in small businesses. Children also worked as domestic servants and endured long work hours and abuse by employers. Children were subjected to commercial sexual exploitation (see section 6, Children) and were recruited into illegal gangs to perform illicit activities related to the arms and drug trades, including homicide.

Also see the Department of Labor's *Findings on the Worst Forms of Child Labor*.

d. Acceptable Conditions of Work

There is no national minimum wage; the minimum wage is determined sector-bysector. The minimum monthly wage was $224.29 for retail and service employees, $219.40 for industrial laborers, and $187.68 for apparel assembly workers. The agricultural minimum wage was $104.97 per month, although some agricultural workers, including coffee workers, were paid by the amount harvested rather than a daily wage. The government reported that the poverty income level was $174.73 for urban areas and $133.82 for rural areas.

The law sets a maximum normal workweek of 44 hours, limited to no more than six days, and to no more than eight hours per day, but allows overtime if a bonus is paid. The law mandates that full-time employees be paid for an eight-hour day of rest in addition to the 44-hour normal workweek. The law provides that employers must pay double time for work on designated annual holidays, a Christmas bonus based on the time of service of the employee, and 15 days of paid annual leave. The law prohibits compulsory overtime. The law states that domestic employees are obligated to render services on holidays if their employer makes this request, but they are entitled to double pay in these instances.

The Ministry of Labor is responsible for setting workplace safety standards, and the law establishes a tripartite committee to review the standards. The law requires all employers to take steps to ensure that employees are not placed at risk to their health and safety in the workplace. The law requires that employers provide preventive safety measures, including proper equipment and training, and a violence-free workplace, in order to reasonably ensure the safety and health of workers. Employers who violate the law can be fined, although penalties were often insufficient to deter violations, and some companies reportedly found it more cost effective to pay the fines rather than comply with the law. The law promotes occupational safety awareness, training, and worker participation in occupational health and safety matters.

The Ministry of Labor was charged with enforcing the law. The government reportedly enforced effectively the minimum wage law in the formal sector, but not in the informal sector, and unions reported that the ministry also failed to enforce the minimum wage for subcontracted workers hired for public reconstruction contracts. There were 202 labor inspectors. The government provided its inspectors updated training in both occupational safety and labor standards. The Ministry of Labor did not provide information on the number of inspections conducted. Allegations of corruption among labor inspectors continued.

The ministry received complaints regarding failure to pay overtime, minimum wage violations, unpaid salaries, as well as cases of employers illegally withholding benefits (including social security and pension funds) from workers. As of August 28, the FGR investigated 557 cases of alleged illegally withheld benefits, though the number of convictions was not available.

According to the Ministry of Labor, immigrant workers have the same rights as Salvadorans, but the ministry did not enforce these rights in practice. There were reports of overtime and wage violations in several sectors. According to the ministry, employers in the agriculture sector did not grant annual bonuses, vacation days, or days of rest. Women in domestic service and the maquila industry, particularly in the export processing zones, faced exploitation, mistreatment, verbal abuse, threats, sexual harassment, and generally poor work conditions. Workers in the construction industry and domestic service were reportedly subject to violations of wage, hour, and safety laws. There were also reports of occupational safety and health violations in other sectors.

In some cases the country's high crime rate negatively affected acceptable conditions of work, as well as workers' psychological and physical health. Some workers, such as bus drivers, bill collectors, messengers, and teachers in high-risk areas, reported being subject to extortion and death threats. According to the Ministry of Economy, in 2011, 49.3 percent of the economically active population worked in the informal economy.

As of October 18, the Ministry of Labor reported 4,002 workplace accidents; 714 accidents occurred in real estate and construction-related businesses, 467 in the textile sector; and 456 in the food and beverage sector.

In: El Salvador
Editor: Joelle Foster

ISBN: 978-1-63321-766-9
© 2014 Nova Science Publishers, Inc.

Chapter 4

EL SALVADOR 2012 INTERNATIONAL RELIGIOUS FREEDOM REPORT[*]

U.S. Department of State; Bureau of Democracy, Human Rights and Labor

EXECUTIVE SUMMARY

The constitution and other laws and policies protect religious freedom and, in practice, the government generally respected religious freedom. The trend in the government's respect for religious freedom did not change significantly during the year.

There were no reports of societal abuses or discrimination based on religious affiliation, belief, or practice.

U.S. embassy officials met periodically with government officials, religious leaders, and university officials to discuss religious freedom.

SECTION I. RELIGIOUS DEMOGRAPHY

According to the National Directorate of Census and Statistics of the Ministry of the Economy, the population is approximately 6.2 million.

---

[*] This is an edited, reformatted and augmented version of a report released by the U.S. Department of State; Bureau of Democracy, Human Rights and Labor, dated May 2013.

According to a May survey by the Institute of Public Opinion of the University of Central America, 47 percent identifies as Roman Catholic and 33 percent as evangelical. The survey reported 17 percent as having "no religion." There are small numbers of Jehovah's Witnesses, Hare Krishnas, Muslims, Jews, Buddhists, and members of The Church of Jesus Christ of Latter-day Saints (Mormons). A small segment of the population adheres to indigenous religious beliefs.

SECTION II. STATUS OF GOVERNMENT RESPECT FOR RELIGIOUS FREEDOM LEGAL/POLICY FRAMEWORK

The constitution and other laws and policies protect religious freedom. The constitution states that all persons are equal before the law and prohibits discrimination based on nationality, race, gender, or religion.

The penal code imposes criminal sentences of six months to two years on those who publicly offend or insult the religious beliefs of others, or damage or destroy religious objects. If such acts are carried out with and for the purpose of publicity, sentences increase to one to three years in prison. Repeat offenders face prison sentences of three to eight years. There have been no prosecutions under this law.

The constitution requires the president, cabinet ministers, vice ministers, supreme court justices, judges, governors, the attorney general, the public defender, and other senior government officials to be laypersons. In addition, the electoral code requires judges of the Supreme Electoral Tribunal and members of municipal councils to be laypersons.

The constitution grants official recognition to the Catholic Church and states that other religious groups may also apply for official recognition. The law grants tax-exempt status to all officially recognized religious groups. Regulations also make donations to officially recognized religious groups tax-deductible.

The civil code grants equal status to churches and nonprofit foundations. For religious groups, registration with the government confers legal recognition as a religious organization. Although religious groups may carry out religious activities without registering with the government, registration makes it easier to conduct activities requiring official permits, such as building churches. To obtain official recognition, a religious group must apply through the Office of the Director General for Nonprofit Associations and Foundations

(DGFASFL) within the Ministry of Governance. The group must present its constitution and bylaws describing the type of organization, location of its offices, its goals and principles, requirements for membership, function of its ruling bodies, and assessments or dues. Before the DGFASFL grants registration, it must determine that the group's constitution and bylaws do not violate the law. Once a group is registered as a nonprofit religious organization, notice of DGFASFL approval and the group's constitution and bylaws must be published in the official gazette. The DGFASFL does not maintain records on religious groups once it approves their status.

By law, the Ministry of Governance has authority to register, regulate, and oversee the finances of nongovernmental organizations (NGOs), non-Catholic churches, and other religious groups. The law specifically exempts the Catholic Church from the registration requirement. As of November, there were 175 new requests for registration of religious groups, of which 108 were approved, 64 were pending, two were withdrawn voluntarily, and one was deferred for lack of response from the applicants. None was denied.

Noncitizens present in the country primarily to proselytize must obtain a special residence visa for religious activities and may not proselytize while on a visitor or tourist visa.

Public education is secular. Private religious schools operate freely. All private schools, whether religious or secular, must meet the same standards to obtain Ministry of Education approval.

The government observes the following religious holidays as national holidays: Maundy Thursday, Good Friday, Holy Saturday, All Souls Day, and Christmas.

Government Practices

There were no reports of abuses of religious freedom.

SECTION III. STATUS OF SOCIETAL RESPECT FOR RELIGIOUS FREEDOM

There were no reports of societal abuses or discrimination based on religious affiliation, belief, or practice. Catholic, Lutheran, Anglican, Baptist, evangelical, Islamic, Jewish, and Buddhist leaders participated in the Council of Religions for Peace. The Council organized events promoting anti-crime initiatives and environmental awareness and conducted prison visits.

SECTION IV. U.S. GOVERNMENT POLICY

U.S. embassy officials met with the assistant ombudsman for civil rights, who reported that his office received no complaints about violations of religious freedom during the year. Embassy officials reviewed the registration process for religious groups with the director general for nonprofit associations and foundations at the Ministry of Governance. Senior embassy officials, including the ambassador and deputy chief of mission, met with leaders of religious groups to discuss religious freedom and security issues. Embassy officials also discussed religious freedom with the director of the Human Rights Institute of the University of Central America as well as representatives of indigenous religious groups.

In: El Salvador
Editor: Joelle Foster

ISBN: 978-1-63321-766-9
© 2014 Nova Science Publishers, Inc.

Chapter 5

2014 INVESTMENT CLIMATE STATEMENT: EL SALVADOR[*]

Bureau of Economic and Business Affairs

EXECUTIVE SUMMARY

El Salvador is eager to attract greater foreign investment and is taking steps to improve its investment climate. In recent years, El Salvador has lagged the region in terms of attraction of Foreign Direct Investment (FDI). The Central Bank of El Salvador reported that FDI reached just $140.0 million in 2013, a 71 percent decline from the $481.9 million received in 2012. Political uncertainty, burdensome commercial regulations, a sometimes ineffective judicial system, and widespread violent crime are often cited as elements that impede investment in El Salvador.

In 2011, El Salvador and the United States initiated the Partnership for Growth (PFG), a new cooperative development model, to help improve El Salvador's economy and investment climate. November 2013 marked the second anniversary of PFG implementation, and the partnership has taken steps to foster a more favorable environment for business and investment, and improve human capital and infrastructure. For more information on PFG, please access the link on the Embassy's website at http://sansalvador.usembassy.gov/.

---

[*] This is an edited, reformatted and augmented version of a report issued by the U.S. Department of State, June 2014.

CAFTA-DR, the free trade agreement among Central American countries, the Dominican Republic, and the United States, entered into force for the United States and El Salvador in 2006. El Salvador also has free trade agreements with Mexico, Chile, Panama, Colombia, and Taiwan. All have entered into force with the exception of the FTA with Colombia which is expected to be activated soon. El Salvador, jointly with Costa Rica, Guatemala, Honduras, Nicaragua, and Panama, signed an Association Agreement with the European Union that includes the establishment of a Free Trade Area. El Salvador is also negotiating trade agreements with Canada, Peru, and Belize.

In October 2012, the Salvadoran government presented to the Legislative Assembly a package of legislation to promote investment and facilitate commerce. Some of these laws have been passed including reforms to the International Services Law and Free Trade Zone Law, and the Construction Simplification Law. In April 2014, the Legislative Assembly approved reforms to address shortcomings in a Public-Private Partnership (PPP) Law that was originally passed in May 2013. The law and associated reforms were designed to provide a legal framework for the development of PPP projects and create a more suitable environment for investment.

1. OPENNESS TO, AND RESTRICTIONS UPON, FOREIGN INVESTMENT

El Salvador is eager to attract greater foreign investment and is taking steps to improve its investment climate. The Central Bank of El Salvador reported that foreign direct investment (FDI) reached just $140.0 million in 2013, a 71 percent decline from the $481.9 million received in 2012. Meanwhile, El Salvador's regional neighbors have experienced generally increasing levels of FDI in recent years, attracting on average more than $1.4 billion per country in 2013.

Political uncertainty, inconsistent and burdensome commercial regulations, a sometimes ineffective judicial system, and widespread violent crime undermine El Salvador's investment climate. CAFTA-DR, the free trade agreement among Central American countries, the Dominican Republic, and the United States, includes an investment chapter and other provisions that have strengthened investment dispute resolution for member state companies with interests in El Salvador.

In 2011, El Salvador and the United States initiated the Partnership for Growth (PFG), a new cooperative development model that aligns complementary commitments by both governments. November 2013 marked the second anniversary of PFG implementation, and the partnership has taken steps to foster a more favorable environment for business and investment, and improve human capital and infrastructure. For more information on PFG, please access the link on the Embassy's website at http://sansalvador.usembassy.gov/.

In October 2012, the Salvadoran government presented to the Legislative Assembly a package of legislation to promote investment and facilitate commerce. Some of these laws have been passed including reforms to the International Services Law and Free Trade Zone Law, and the Construction Simplification Law. Other key proposed legislation such as the Judicial Stability Law for Investments and Electronic Signature Law have not been passed.

In April 2014, the Legislative Assembly approved reforms to address shortcomings in the country's Public-Private Partnership (PPP) Law which was originally passed in May 2013. The law and associated reforms were designed to provide a legal framework for the development of PPP projects and create a more suitable environment for investment.

The existing 1999 Investment Law grants equal treatment to foreign and domestic investors. With the exception of micro businesses (ten or fewer employees and sales of less than $68,571/year), foreign investors may freely establish businesses in El Salvador. Investors who begin operations with ten or fewer employees must present plans to increase employment to the Ministry of Economy's National Investment Office (ONI). The Investment Law also provides that underground resources (minerals) belong to the state. The state may grant concessions for their extraction, but there have been no new permits for mineral extraction in recent years. Per the constitution, rural property cannot be acquired by foreigners from countries where Salvadorans do not enjoy the same right unless it is used for industrial purposes.

Additional statues governing foreign investment in El Salvador include the Export Reactivation Law, the International Services Law, and Free Trade Zone Law. Other statutes establishing the basic legal framework for investment include the Public Private Partnership Law, Monetary Integration Law, Banking Law, Insurance Companies Law, Securities Market Law, Competition Law, Tourism Law, intellectual property laws, and special legislation governing privatizations and credit cards.

FDI inflows to El Salvador originate from across the globe, including from the United States, Panama, Mexico, Spain, Canada, Costa Rica, Guatemala, Germany, and Italy, and target a variety of sectors of the economy.

Aeronautics: For the past several years El Salvador has promoted itself as a promising logistics and transportation center and aeronautics cluster for the region. El Salvador's international airport is a hub for Colombian airline, Avianca, and home to an international commercial aircraft maintenance, repair and overhaul facility, Aeroman. The government is developing plans to modernize and expand El Salvador's international airport.

Banking: El Salvador's banking sector includes a high concentration of foreign ownership. Ten private sector banks (non-state owned) account for roughly 95 percent of the industry's loan portfolio, two state-owned banks hold about 4 percent, and seven cooperatives and savings and loans make up the rest.

Table 1. El Salvador's Lending Institutions (excluding Salvadoran cooperatives and savings and loans)

Ranking (based on outstanding loans)	Banking Institution	Ownership
1	Banco Agrícola, S.A.	Private, Colombian
2	Scotiabank El Salvador, S.A.	Private, Canadian
3	Banco Davivienda Salvadoreño, S. A.	Private, Colombian
4	Banco Citibank de El Salvador, S.A.	Private, United States
5	Banco de América Central, S.A.	Private, Colombian
6	Banco Promérica, S.A.	Private, Salvadoran
7	Banco Hipotecario de El Salvador, S.A.	State-owned, Salvadoran
8	Banco G&T Continental El Salvador, S.A.	Private, Guatemalan
9	Banco Procredit, S.A.	Private, Salvadoran
10	Banco de Fomento Agropecuario	State-owned, Salvadoran
11	Banco Industrial El Salvador, S.A.	Private, Guatemalan
12	Banco Azteca El Salvador, S.A.	Private, Mexican

Construction: The Construction Permit Simplification Law, approved by the Legislative Assembly in October 2013, reduces processing costs and waiting times for permits (environmental, public works, municipal offices, etc.) for real estate developers by providing a one-stop window for all processes and permits. It also establishes a time horizon by which the government entities must react to a permit application or the permit will be considered approved.

Energy: To address the country's high electricity costs and growing energy needs, El Salvador awarded a contract in December 2013 to a local consortium to build a 355 megawatt Liquefied Natural Gas (LNG) plant near the Port of Acajutla. This estimated $1 billion project would increase the country's total energy generation capacity by 20 percent and, if completed on schedule, would be operational by 2018. In 2013, El Salvador launched two renewable energy solicitations for 15 megawatts and 100 megawatts of solar and wind projects to diversify its energy matrix and reduce the country's dependence on fuel oil. A major international energy company has an ongoing dispute with the Salvadoran government over its geothermal operations in El Salvador (see section "Competition from State Owned Enterprises").

Media and Telecommunications: Privatization and foreign investment have helped to modernize Salvadoran media and telecommunications. The only remaining restrictions for foreign investors are on free reception television and AM/FM radio broadcasting, where foreign ownership cannot exceed 49 percent of equity. There has been extensive growth in the cellular phone industry. In 2012, Mexican-owned America Móvil attempted to expand its operations by purchasing one of the five major service providers, but abandoned its bid after the Salvadoran anti-trust authority required it give up some of its existing spectrum. Additionally, El Salvador is making preliminary plans to switch to digital television.

Services: The January 2013 reforms to the International Services Law added industries eligible for special incentives: container repair and maintenance, technology equipment repair, elderly and convalescent care, telemedicine, and cinematography. The reforms also allow operation outside of designated service parks and free zones and provide additional incentives for existing firms that expand into new services. The call center industry has experienced particularly strong growth in El Salvador over the last several years. Currently, five of the country's top 25 employers (based on number of employees) are call centers. The government is also promoting other service sectors such as software design and animation, architectural design, and medical tourism.

Textiles, Apparel, and free trade zone activities: El Salvador's free trade zones host many international textile and apparel firms, including Fruit of the Loom and Hanesbrands. The February 2013 reforms to the Free Trade Zone Law made it compliant with World Trade Organization (WTO) regulations. The reforms eliminate permanent tax exemptions based on export performance and instead grant tax credits based on number of employees and investment levels.

TABLE 2B – Scorecards: The Millennium Challenge Corporation, a U.S. Government entity charged with delivering development grants to countries that have demonstrated a commitment to reform produced scorecards for countries with a 2012 per capita gross national income (GCI) of $ 4,085 or less. A list of countries with MCC scorecards and links to those scorecards is available here: http://www.mcc.gov/pages/selection/scorecards. Details on each of the MCC's indicators and a guide to reading the scorecards are available here: http://www.mcc.gov/documents/reports/reference-20130011 42401-fy14-guide-to-the- indicators.pdf.

2. CONVERSION AND TRANSFER POLICIES

There are no restrictions on transferring funds associated with investment out of the country. Foreign businesses can freely remit or reinvest profits, repatriate capital, and bring in capital for additional investment. The 1999 Investment Law allows unrestricted remittance of royalties and fees from the use of foreign patents, trademarks, technical assistance, and other services. Tax reforms introduced in 2011, however, levy a five percent tax on national or foreign shareholders' profits. Moreover, shareholders domiciled in a state, country or territory with low or no taxes or that is considered a tax haven, will instead be subject to a tax of twenty-five percent.

The Monetary Integration Law dollarized El Salvador in 2001, and the U.S. dollar now freely circulates and can be used in all transactions. One objective of dollarization was to make El Salvador more attractive to foreign investors. U.S. dollars account for nearly all currency in circulation. Salvadoran banks, in accordance with the law, must keep all accounts in dollars. Dollarization is supported by family remittances -- almost all from the United States -- that totaled $4 billion in 2013.

Table 2. El Salvador's Economic Rankings

Measure	Year	Ranking / Score	Website Address
WEF Global Competitiveness	2013	97 out of 148	http://www3.weforum.org/ docs/ GCR2013-14/GCR_ Rankings_2013-14.pdf
Transparency Int'l Corruption Index	2013	83 out of 177	http://cpi.transparency.org/ cpi2013/results/
Heritage Foundation's Economic Freedom index	2014	59 out of 178	http://www.heritage.org/ index/ranking
World Bank's Doing Business Report	2014	118 out of 189	http://www.doingbusiness. org/rankings

3. EXPROPRIATION AND COMPENSATION

El Salvador's 1983 constitution allows the government to expropriate private property for reasons of public utility or social interest, and indemnification can take place either before or after the fact. There are no recent cases of expropriation. In 1980, a rural/agricultural land reform established that no single natural or legal person could own more than 245 hectares (605 acres) of land, and the government expropriated the land of some large landholders. While banks were nationalized in 1980, beginning in 1990 they were returned to private ownership. A 2003 amendment to the 1996 Electricity Law contains a provision that, while not authorizing expropriation, requires energy generating companies to obtain government approval before removing fixed capital from the country. According to the Salvadoran government, this provision is intended to prevent energy supply disruptions.

In 2009, the U.S. subsidiary of Pacific Rim, a Canadian mining company, filed an international arbitration proceeding against the Salvadoran government alleging various violations of the obligations in Chapter Ten of the CAFTA-DR. Pacific Rim (since purchased in November 2013 by OceanaGold Corporation headquartered in Australia) alleged that the Salvadoran government wrongfully refused to grant environmental permits for its mineral extraction projects. In June 2012, the CAFTA-DR claims were dismissed because the International Center for Settlement of Investment Disputes (ICSID) tribunal determined the U.S. subsidiary lacked substantial business activities in the United States to qualify as a party under CAFTA-DR.

The tribunal found, however, that it did have jurisdiction to proceed on an evaluation of the merits of the firm's claims under Salvadoran investment law. The case is ongoing.

4. DISPUTE SETTLEMENT

While foreign investors can seek redress of commercial disputes through Salvadoran courts, some investors have found the slow-moving domestic legal system to be costly and unproductive. The course of some cases has shown that the legal system is subject to manipulation by various interests, and final rulings are sometimes not enforced. Where possible, arbitration clauses, preferably with a foreign venue, should be included in commercial contracts as a means to resolve business disputes. Investors should make sure that all contracts are carefully drafted and that relationships with local firms are specifically defined. Some U.S. firms have been embroiled in legal disputes in recent years. In some cases, multinational firms asserted that a contract with a Salvadoran firm had either formally ended or never existed, but Salvadoran courts ruled that the contract remained in force. Local investment and commercial dispute resolution proceedings in El Salvador routinely last many years.

El Salvador's commercial law is based on the Commercial Code and the Code for Mercantile Processes. There is a mercantile court system for resolving commercial disputes, although parties have complained about its slow processes and erratic rulings, particularly at the Supreme Court level. The Commercial Code, Code of Mercantile Processes, and Banking Law contain sections that deal with bankruptcy but there is no separate bankruptcy law or court. In 2008, the Legislative Assembly passed several reforms to the Commercial Code and the Commerce Registry Law. The reforms were aimed to facilitate trade and investment by reducing the number of steps and requirements to register, develop, and close a business. As a result of the reforms, all documents and payments can be submitted electronically to the Commerce Registry.

Article 15 of the 1999 Investment Law was reformed in August 2013. As revised, the law limits the access of foreign investors originating from a country without a pre-existing trade agreement to international dispute resolution and may oblige them to use national courts. The rights of investors from CAFTA-DR countries appear to be protected under the trade agreement's dispute settlement procedures. Submissions to national dispute panels and panel hearings are open to the public, and interested parties have the opportunity to register their views. In addition, in 2002, the government approved a law that allowed private sector organizations to establish arbitration centers for the resolution of commercial disputes, including those involving foreign investors.

In 2009, El Salvador modified its arbitration law to allow parties to arbitration disputes the ability to appeal a ruling to the Salvadoran courts. Investors have complained that the modification dilutes the fundamental efficacy of arbitration as an alternative method of resolving disputes.

5. PERFORMANCE REQUIREMENTS AND INVESTMENT INCENTIVES

El Salvador's Investment Law does not require investors to meet export targets, transfer technology, incorporate a specific percentage of local content, or fulfill other performance criteria. Foreign investors and domestic firms are eligible for the same incentives. Exports of goods and services are levied zero value added tax.

The 1998 Free Trade Zone Law is designed to attract investment in a wide range of activities, although at present the vast majority of the businesses in export processing zones are clothing assembly plants. A Salvadoran partner is not needed to operate in a free trade zone, and some textile operations are completely foreign-owned.

The 1998 law established rules for export processing zones (free zones) and bonded areas. The free zones are outside the nation's customs jurisdiction while the bonded areas are within its jurisdiction but subject to special treatment. Local and foreign companies can establish themselves in a free zone to produce goods or services for export or to provide services linked to international trade. The regulations for the bonded areas are similar.

The February 2013 reforms to the Free Trade Zone Law made it compliant with World Trade Organization (WTO) regulations. The reforms eliminate permanent tax exemptions based on export performance and instead grant tax credits based on number of employees and investment levels. Qualifying firms located in the free zones and bonded areas may enjoy the following benefits:

    a. Exemption from all duties and taxes on imports of raw materials and the machinery and equipment needed to produce for export;

- b. Exemption from taxes for fuels and lubricants used for producing exports if these are not domestically produced;
- c. Exemption from income tax, municipal taxes on company assets and property; the exemptions are for 15 years if the company is located in the metropolitan area of San Salvador and for 20 years if the company is located outside of the metropolitan area of San Salvador. After that, the user would still be able to obtain partial exemptions.
- d. Exemption from taxes on real estate transfers for the acquisition of goods to be employed in the authorized activity.

Companies in the free zones are also allowed to sell goods or services in the Salvadoran market if they pay applicable taxes for the proportion sold locally. Additional rules apply to textile and apparel products.

Under the 1990 Export Reactivation Law, firms were able to apply for tax rebates ("drawbacks") of six percent of the FOB value of manufactured or processed exports shipped outside the Central American Common Market area. This benefit was eliminated in 2011. However, later that same year the Salvadoran government approved new regulations to support producers. The regulations include a new form of "drawback," approved by the World Trade Organization (WTO), which consists of a refund of custom duties paid on imported inputs and intermediate goods exclusively used in the production of goods exported outside of the Central American region. The new regulations also include the creation of a Business Production Promotion Committee with the participation of the private and public sector to work on policies to strengthen the export sector, and the creation of an Export and Import Center. Since 2011, all import and export procedures are handled by the Export and Import Center. More information about the procedures can be found at: https://www.centrex.gob.sv/

The International Services Law, approved in 2007, establishes service parks and centers with incentives similar to those received by El Salvador's free trade zones. Service park developers may be exempted from income tax for 15 years, municipal taxes for ten years, and real estate transfer taxes. Service park administrators will be exempted from income tax for 15 years and from municipal taxes for ten years. Firms located in the service parks/service centers may receive the following permanent benefits:

- a. Tariff exemption for the import of capital goods, machinery, equipment, tools, supplies, accessories, furniture and other goods needed for the development of the service activities (goods and

services such as food and beverages, tobacco products, alcoholic beverages, rental fees, home equipment and furniture, cleaning articles, luxury goods, transportation vehicles, and hotel services are not exempted from taxation);
b. Full and indefinite exemption from income tax and municipal taxes on company assets.

Service firms operating under the existing Free Trade Zone Law are also covered. However, if the services are provided to the Salvadoran market, they cannot receive the benefits of the International Services Law.

The following services are covered under the International Services Law: international distribution, logistical international operations, call centers, information technology, research and development, marine vessels repair and maintenance, aircraft repair and maintenance, entrepreneurial processes (i.e., business process outsourcing), hospital-medical services, international financial services, container repair and maintenance, technology equipment repair, elderly and convalescent care, telemedicine, and cinematography postproduction services.

To qualify for benefits, businesses must invest at least $150,000 during the first year of operations, including working capital and fixed assets, must hire no fewer than 10 permanent employees, and must have at least a one-year contract. For hospital/medical services, the minimum investment in fixed assets must be $10 million if surgical services are provided or a minimum of $3 million if surgical services are not provided. Hospital or medical services must be located outside of major metropolitan areas. The medical service must also be provided only to patients with insurance.

In 2005, the government approved a tourism law to spur investment in the sector. The law establishes fiscal incentives for those who invest a minimum of $50,000 in tourism-related projects in El Salvador. Incentives include a ten-year income tax exemption and no duties on imports of capital and other goods, subject to some limitations. The investor also benefits from a five-year exemption from land acquisition taxes and a 50 percent break in municipal taxes. To take advantage of these incentives, the enterprise must contribute five percent of profits during the exemption period to a government-administered Tourism Promotion Fund.

Those who plan to live and work in El Salvador for an extended period will need to obtain temporary residency, which may be renewed periodically. Under Article 11 of the Investment Law, foreigners with investments equal to or more than 4,000 minimum monthly wages ($969,600) have the right to receive Investor's Residence, permitting them to work and stay in the country. Such residency can be requested within 30 days after the investment has been registered. The residency permit covers the investor and his family and is issued for one year, subject to extension on a yearly basis.

Most companies employ a local lawyer to manage the process of obtaining residency. The American Chamber of Commerce in El Salvador can also help its members with the process. Labor regulations require that 90 percent of the labor force at plants and in clerical jobs be Salvadoran. There are fewer nationality restrictions on professional and technical jobs.

U.S. companies have complained of variable customs valuations and inconsistent enforcement of both customs regulations and CAFTA-DR preferential treatment for goods coming from CAFTA-DR countries aside from the United States. While advances have been made to implement a fast-track system for shipments via express courier companies, it has not been fully implemented. The clearance procedures for samples which arrive via express shipments are still an ongoing issue.

6. RIGHT TO PRIVATE OWNERSHIP AND ESTABLISHMENT

No single natural or legal person--Salvadoran or foreign--can own more than 245 hectares (605 acres). Per the constitution, rural property cannot be acquired by foreigners from countries where Salvadorans do not enjoy the same right unless it is used for industrial purposes. Foreign citizens and private companies can freely establish businesses in El Salvador. The only exception for this is in some cases involving small business. A 2001 fishing law allows foreigners to engage in commercial fishing anywhere in Salvadoran waters providing they obtain a license from CENDEPESCA, a government entity.

7. PROTECTION OF PROPERTY RIGHTS

Private property, both non-real estate and real estate, is recognized and protected in El Salvador. Companies that plan to buy land or other real estate are advised to conduct a thorough search of the property's title prior to purchase.

In 2005, El Salvador revised several laws to comply with CAFTA-DR's provisions on intellectual property rights (IPR). The Intellectual Property Promotion and Protection Law (1993, revised in 2005), Law of Trademarks and Other Distinctive Signs (2002, revised in 2005), and Penal Code establish the legal framework to protect IPR. Investors can register trademarks, patents, copyrights, and other forms of intellectual property with the National Registry Center's Intellectual Property Office.

Reforms passed in 2005 extended the copyright term from 50 to 70 years. In 2008, the government enacted test data exclusivity regulations for pharmaceuticals and agrochemicals, which will be protected for 5 and 10 years respectively, and ratified an international agreement extending protection to satellite signals.

In March 2012, El Salvador passed a new Medicines Law to regulate the production, sale, and distribution of pharmaceuticals. The law created the National Directorate of Medicines to oversee implementation, including the drafting of new regulations and establishment of price controls on the sale of pharmaceuticals. The new regulations were published by the Directorate in December 2012.

The Attorney General's office and the National Civilian Police enforce trademark and intellectual rights by conducting raids against distributors and manufacturers of pirated CDs, cassettes, clothes, and computer software. The 2005 reforms authorize the seizure, forfeiture, and destruction of counterfeit and pirated goods and the equipment used to produce them. They also allow authorities to initiate these raids ex-officio, and piracy is now punishable by jail sentences of two to six years. However, using the criminal and mercantile courts to seek redress of a violation of intellectual property is often a slow and frustrating process.

Judiciary and regulatory enforcement continue to be the weakest pillars of intellectual property protection in El Salvador. A significant intellectual property rights case continues to drag through the Salvadoran courts concerning a contractual dispute between McDonald's and an ex- franchisee involving trademark and copyright infringement. In October 2011, the Salvadoran Supreme Court upheld a previous award of $24 million to the ex-franchisee. McDonald's continued appeals. In October 2012, the Supreme Court again decided in favor of the ex- franchiser and McDonald's paid an award, though further legal issues remain.

El Salvador is a signatory of the Bern Convention for the Protection of Literary and Artistic Works; the Paris Convention for the Protection of Industrial Property; the Geneva Convention for the Protection of Producers of

Phonograms Against Unauthorized Duplication; the World Intellectual Property Organization (WIPO) Copyright Treaty; the WIPO Performance and Phonograms Treaty; and the Rome Convention for the Protection of Performers, Phonogram Producers, and Broadcasting Organizations.

For additional information about treaty obligations and points of contact at local IP offices, please see WIPO's country profiles at http://www.wipo.int/directory/en/.

Embassy point of contact: san.salvador.office.box@mail.doc.gov

Local lawyers list: http://sansalvador.usembassy.gov/local-information/list-of-attorneys.html

8. TRANSPARENCY OF THE REGULATORY SYSTEM

The laws and regulations of El Salvador are relatively transparent and generally foster competition. However, the government does control the price of some goods and services, including electricity, liquid propane gas, gasoline, fares on public transport, and medicines. The government also directly subsidizes water services and sets the distribution-service tariff.

Bureaucratic procedures have improved in recent years and are relatively streamlined for foreign investors. Regulatory agencies, however, are often understaffed and inexperienced, especially when dealing with complex issues. New foreign investors should review the regulatory environment carefully.

The Superintendent of Electricity and Telecommunications (SIGET) oversees electricity rates, telecommunications, and distribution of electromagnetic frequencies.

In 2003, the government amended the 1996 Electricity Law with the intention of reducing volatility in the wholesale market and thereby stabilizing retail electricity prices and encouraging new investment. The new reforms to the law allowed SIGET to develop a cost-based pricing model for the electricity sector, which they introduced to the marketplace in 2011. The new system requires the adoption of additional long-term contracts and should alleviate various market distortions. The Salvadoran Government subsidizes consumers using up to 200 kWh monthly. The electricity subsidy costs the government upwards of $185 million annually. Energy sector companies have warned that ever-changing subsidies and the government's inability to pay the subsidies in a timely manner have eroded the financial stability of the power sector and discouraged needed investment in new generation capacity.

The 2004 Competition Law defines a series of anticompetitive practices such as collusion to fix prices, limit production, and rig bids. Vertical arrangements, tying (conditioning the sale of one product on the sale of another), and exclusive dealing are also outlawed. Certain abuses of dominant market position are also prohibited, for example, creating barriers to entry by other firms, predatory pricing to drive out competitors, price discrimination and similar actions when intended to limit competition are illegal. The law created an autonomous Superintendent of Competition responsible for enforcing the law. The Superintendent of Competition's decisions, particularly against gasoline and energy companies, have resulted in a series of lawsuits filed against the El Salvadoran government.

El Salvador is a member of the U.N. Conference on Trade and Development's international network of transparent investment procedures: http://elsalvador.eregulations.org/. Foreign and national investors can find detailed information on administrative procedures applicable to investment and income generating operations including the number of steps, name and contact details of the entities and persons in charge of procedures, required documents and conditions, costs, processing time, and legal bases justifying the procedures.

9. EFFICIENT CAPITAL MARKETS AND PORTFOLIO INVESTMENT

The Superintendent of the Financial System supervises individual and consolidated activities of banks and non-bank financial intermediaries, financial conglomerates, stock market participants, insurance companies, and pension fund administrators. Interest rates are determined by market forces and have decreased significantly since dollarization was implemented. Foreign investors may obtain credit in the local financial market under the same conditions as local investors. Accounting systems are generally consistent with international norms.

In February 2013, a new Usury Law entered into force to regulate interest rates on credit cards and loans provided by banking institutions, commercial establishments, stores, credit card issuers, pawnshops, cooperatives, credit unions, and private lenders. According to the legislation, the maximum interest rate for credit cards and loans would be 1.6 times the simple average effective rate established by the Central Bank.

El Salvador's banks are among the largest in Central America and many are owned by foreign financial institutions. The banking system is sound and generally well-managed and supervised. The banking system's total assets as of March 2014 totaled $14.4 billion.

Under the 1999 Banking Law and amendments made in 2002, foreign banks are afforded national treatment and can offer the same services as Salvadoran banks. The law strengthened supervisory authorities and provided more transparent and secure operations for customers and banks. The law also established an FDIC-like autonomous institution to insure deposits, increased minimum capital reserve requirements, and sharply limited bank lending to shareholders and directors.

The Non-Bank Financial Intermediaries Law regulates the organization, operation, and activities of financial institutions such as cooperative savings associations, nongovernmental organizations, and other microfinance institutions. The Money Laundering Law requires financial institutions to report suspicious transactions to the Attorney General and the Superintendent of the Financial System.

The 1996 Insurance Companies Law regulates the operation of local insurance firms and accords national treatment to foreign insurance firms. Foreign firms, including U.S., Colombian, Canadian, and Spanish companies, have invested in Salvadoran insurers.

The 1994 Securities Market Law established the present framework for the Salvadoran securities exchange, which opened in 1992. The Salvadoran securities exchange has played an important role in past years in the privatization of state enterprises and more recently in securitizations and facilitating foreign portfolio investment. Stocks, government and private bonds, and other financial instruments are traded on the exchange, which is regulated by the Superintendent of the Financial System.

Foreigners may buy stocks, bonds, and other instruments sold on the exchange and may have their own securities listed, once approved by the Superintendent. Companies interested in listing must first register with the National Registry Center's Registry of Commerce.

Between 2012 and 2013, the exchange averaged daily trading volumes of about $14.3 million. Government-regulated private pension funds, Salvadoran insurance companies, and local banks are the largest buyers on the Salvadoran securities exchange.

In 2007, the Legislative Assembly approved a Securitization Law. There have been a number of transactions worth between $10 to 50 million executed under the Securitization Law and there are at least two firms authorized to underwrite securitizations.

10. COMPETITION FROM STATE-OWNED ENTERPRISES

El Salvador has successfully liberalized many sectors where the government previously exerted monopoly control, effectively limiting most forms of direct competition from state-owned enterprises. While energy distribution was privatized in 1999, the Salvadoran Government maintains significant energy production facilities through state-owned Rio Lempa Executive Hydroelectric Commission (CEL), a significant producer of hydro-electric and geothermal energy.

La Geo, a joint venture between CEL and Italian-owned Enel Green Power, has exclusive geothermal rights in El Salvador. New investment in La Geo has been stunted by lengthy legal disputes between the Salvadoran government and Enel. While international arbitration proceedings have ruled in favor of Enel, the Salvadoran Supreme Court ruled in 2012 that the original geothermal concession to La Geo was unconstitutional. In April 2014, the Salvadoran Attorney General issued an order to freeze $2 billion worth of assets belonging to the entities and individuals involved in the pending case surrounding La Geo, including Enel.

Alba Petroleos (AP) is a joint-venture between a consortium of mayors from the left-leaning Farabundo Marti National Liberation Front (FMLN) party and a subsidiary of Venezuela's state-owned oil company PDVSA. AP operates dozens of gasoline service stations across the country and has expanded into a number of other industries, including: energy production, food production, medicines, micro-lending, supermarket, bus transportation, and aviation. Because of its official relationship with the ruling FMLN party, critics have charged that AP receives preferential treatment from the government. Critics have also alleged that AP trade practices, including financial reporting, are non-transparent.

11. CORPORATE SOCIAL RESPONSIBILITY

The private sector in El Salvador, including several prominent U.S. companies, has embraced the concept of corporate social responsibility (CSR).

There are a number of local foundations that promote CSR practices, entrepreneurial values, and philanthropic initiatives. El Salvador is also a member of international institutions such as Forum Empresa (an Alliance of CSR institutions in the Western Hemisphere), AccountAbility (UK), and the InterAmerican CSR Network.

Businesses have created CSR programs in the workplace that provide education and training, transportation, lunch programs, and childcare. In addition, CSR programs have provided assistance to surrounding communities in areas such as health, education, senior housing, and HIV/AIDS awareness.

12. POLITICAL VIOLENCE

El Salvador's 12-year civil war ended in 1992 upon the signing of peace accords. Former guerrilla groups organized themselves into the FMLN party, which has participated in elections since 1994. FMLN candidate Mauricio Funes won the presidential election in March 2009, marking the first transition of power to a left-wing party since the end of the civil war. The FMLN maintained the presidency in March 2014 after a narrow victory for Salvador Sánchez Cerén.

In El Salvador, there has been no political violence aimed at foreign investors, their businesses, or their property.

13. CORRUPTION

U.S. individuals and firms operating or investing in El Salvador should take the time to become familiar with the relevant anticorruption laws in order to properly comply with them, and where appropriate, they should seek the advice of legal counsel. U.S. companies operating in El Salvador are subject to the U.S. Foreign Corrupt Practices Act.

Corruption can be a challenge to investment in El Salvador. El Salvador ranks 83 out of 177 countries in Transparency International's Corruption Perceptions 2013 Index.

El Salvador has laws, regulations and penalties to combat corruption, but their effectiveness is inconsistent. Soliciting, offering, or accepting a bribe is a criminal act in El Salvador.

The Attorney General has a special office, the Anticorruption and Complex Crimes Unit, which handles cases involving corruption by public officials and administrators. The Constitution also established the Court of Accounts that is charged with investigating public officials and entities and, when necessary, passing such cases to the Attorney General for prosecution. In 2005, the government issued a code of ethics for the executive-branch employees, including administrative enforcement mechanisms, and it established an Ethics Tribunal in 2006.

The Legislative Assembly approved a new Transparency Law in 2011 in an effort to combat corruption and increase government accountability. In February 2013, President Funes appointed members to the Access to Information Institute as mandated by the law. The Institute's effectiveness, however, has not been demonstrated.

There have been some recent corruption scandals at the federal, legislative, and municipal levels. There have also been credible complaints of judicial corruption. El Salvador has an active, free press that reports on corruption.

El Salvador is not a signatory to the OECD Convention on Combating Bribery of Foreign Public Officials in International Business Transactions. El Salvador is a signatory to the UN Anticorruption Convention and the Organization of American States' Inter-American Convention Against Corruption.

14. BILATERAL INVESTMENT AGREEMENTS

CAFTA-DR, the free trade agreement among Central American countries, the Dominican Republic, and the United States entered into force for the United States and El Salvador on March 1, 2006. CAFTA-DR's investment chapter provides protection to most categories of investment, including enterprises, debt, concessions, contract, and intellectual property. Under the agreement, U.S. investors enjoy, in almost all circumstances, the right to establish, acquire, and operate investments in El Salvador on an equal footing with local investors. Among the rights afforded to U.S. investors are due process protection and the right to receive a fair market value for property in the event of an expropriation. Investor rights are protected under CAFTA-DR by an effective, impartial procedure for dispute settlement that is fully transparent and open to the public.

In 2010, a new alcohol tax entered into force in El Salvador. U.S. industry has voiced concerns that the new tax discriminates against imported alcohol, in violation of El Salvador's CAFTA- DR and WTO obligations. The El Salvadoran government has not officially confirmed its position on whether the CAFTA-DR is a multilateral agreement versus a bilateral agreement with the United States. U.S. firms have raised concerns that El Salvador may not be adhering to its CAFTA-DR obligations regarding import treatment of goods from free trade zones in other Central American countries which appear to meet CAFTA-DR rules of origin requirements. In addition, the USG has raised CAFTA-DR procurement obligation concerns with respect to the Salvadoran government's corn and bean seed distribution program.

El Salvador also has free trade agreements with Mexico, Chile, Panama, Colombia, and Taiwan. All have entered into force with the exception of the FTA with Colombia which is expected to be activated soon. El Salvador, jointly with Costa Rica, Guatemala, Honduras, Nicaragua, and Panama, signed an Association Agreement with the European Union that includes the establishment of a Free Trade Area. The agreement includes a provision for Central American countries and Panama to get access to a wider range of EU development aid. The agreement was ratified on December 11, 2012 by the European Parliament and entered into force with El Salvador in August 2013. The five Central American Common Market countries, which include El Salvador, have an investment treaty among themselves.

The free trade agreements that El Salvador has with Mexico, Chile, and Panama include investment provisions. El Salvador is also negotiating trade agreements with Canada, Peru, and Belize that will contain investment provisions. The Salvadoran government signed a Partial Scope Agreement (PSA) with Cuba in 2011 and is negotiating another with Ecuador.

15. OPIC AND OTHER INVESTMENT INSURANCE PROGRAMS

The Overseas Private Investment Corporation (OPIC) insures against currency inconvertibility, expropriation, and civil strife and can provide corporate project financing and special financing to small business. OPIC has a bilateral agreement with El Salvador that requires the Salvadoran government to approve all insurance applications. A new agreement is being negotiated that will eliminate this requirement. In 2006, OPIC signed an agreement with the El Salvador's National Investment and Exports Promotion Agency (PROESA) to improve outreach to U.S. small business investors in El Salvador. Because El Salvador uses the U.S. dollar, full inconvertibility insurance may be unnecessary, but investors do insure against inability to transfer funds. El Salvador is a member of the Multilateral Investment Guarantee Agency (MIGA).

16. LABOR

In 2012, El Salvador had a labor force of approximately 2.6 million. While Salvadoran labor is regarded as hard working, general education and professional skill levels are low. According to many large employers, there is also a lack of middle management-level talent, which sometimes results in the necessity to transplant additional managers from abroad. Employers do not report labor-related difficulties in incorporating technology into their workplaces.

The constitution guarantees the right of employees in the private sector to organize into associations and unions. Employers are free to hire union or non-union labor. Closed shops are illegal. Labor law is generally in accordance with internationally recognized standards, but is not enforced consistently by government authorities. In 2011, several businesses expressed concerns about the government's application of labor laws, alleging a disregard of established legal procedures.

17. FOREIGN TRADE ZONES/FREE PORTS

As of April 2014, there were 16 free trade zones operating in El Salvador. They host more than 200 companies operating in areas such as textiles, distribution, call centers, business process outsourcing, agribusiness, agriculture, electronics, and metallurgy. Owned primarily by Salvadoran, U.S., Taiwanese, and Korean investors, the firms employ a labor force of approximately 71,500. The section above on Performance Requirements and Incentives outlines the benefits available to investors in these zones.

18. FOREIGN DIRECT INVESTMENT AND FOREIGN PORTFOLIO INVESTMENT STATISTICS

Table 3. Key Macroeconomic Data, U.S. FDI in El Salvador

Economic Data	Year	Amount	Year	Amount	Source of data
GDP	Central Bank of El Salvador		International Monetary Fund		
El Salvador Gross Domestic Product (GDP) (*Millions U.S. Dollars*)	2013 2012	24,259 23,814	2013 2012	24,512 23,864	• http://www.bcr.gob.sv/bcrsite/?cdr=23&lang=es • http://www.imf.org/external/pubs/ft/weo/2014/01/weodata/weorept.aspx?sy=2009&ey=2013&scsm=1&ssd=1&sort=country&ds=.&br=1&pr1.x=52&pr1.y=7&c=253&s=NGDP&grp=0&a=
Foreign Direct Investment (Stock)	Central Bank of El Salvador		U.S. Bureau of Economic Analysis (BEA)		
U.S. FDI in El Salvador (Millions U.S. Dollars, *stock positions*)	2013 2012	2,344 2,385	2013 2012	pending release 2,697	• http://www.bcr.gob.sv/bcrsite/?cdr=125&lang=es • http://www.bea.gov/international/di1usdbal.htm
U.S. Inbound FDI Stock as % GDP	2013 2012	9.7 10	2013 2012	n/a 11.3	See above.
Foreign Direct Investment (Inflows)	Central Bank of El Salvador		United Nations Economic Commission for Latin America and the Caribbean (ECLAC)		
Total FDI inflows to El Salvador	2013 2012	140.1 481.9	2013 2012	137.2 483.6	• http://www.bcr.gob.sv/bcrsite/?cdr=131&lang=es

Economic Data	Year	Amount	Year	Amount	Source of data
(Millions U.S. Dollars)					• http://interwp.cepal.org/sisgen/ConsultaIntegrada.asp?idIndicador=1824&idioma=i
Total FDI inflows as % GDP	2013	0.6	2013	0.6	See above.
	2012	2.0	2012	2.0	

Table 4. Sources and Destination of FDI (stock)

2012 Direct Investment from/in Counterpart Economy Data (Stocks)					
From Top Five Sources/To Top Five Destinations *(US Dollars, Millions)*					
Inward Direct Investment			Outward Direct Investment		
Total Inward	8,635	100%	Total Outward	6	100%
United States	2,798	32%	Nicaragua	5	88%
Panama	2,465	29%	Guatemala	0	7%
Mexico	820	9%	Costa Rica	0	3%
Virgin Islands, British	493	6%	Honduras	0	2%
Spain	280	3%	United States	0	-1%
"0" reflects amounts rounded to +/- USD 500,000.					

Source: Direct data query from International Monetary Fund, http://cdis.imf.org

Partial List of Major Foreign Investors

AES Corporation (USA) -- Electricity distribution
AIG (USA) -- Insurance
Alba Petroleos (Venezuela) -- Gas station, refinery, electricity generation
Avery Dennison (USA) -- Labeling and packaging
Bancolombia (Colombia) -- Banking
Bayer de El Salvador (German) -- Pharmaceutical processing, fertilizers
Decameron International (Colombia) -- Tourism/hotels
DELSUR (Colombia) -- Electricity distribution
Banco Davivienda -- formerly
HSBC (Colombia) -- Banking
Citigroup (USA) -- Banking
Scotiabank (Canada) -- Banking

Digicel (Caribbean) -- Cellular telephone service
Duke Energy (USA) -- Thermal electricity generation plants
Elf (France) -- Propane gas
Cenergica (Israel) -- Owner/operator of the Nejapa power/generating plant
EMEL S.A. (Chilean/USA) -- Electricity distribution
Trafigura PUMA Energy(Netherlands) -- Gas stations/small refinery at Acajutla
America Movil (Mexico) -- Fixed and wireless telephone, retail
Fruit of the Loom (USA) -- Apparel assembly
Grupo Calvo (Spain) -- Tuna fishing/processing
Hanes Brand (USA) -- Apparel assembly
Holcim (Swiss) -- Cement
Intelfon (Panama/El Salvador) -- Telecommunications
International Paper (USA) -- Packaging
Lacoste (France) -- Textiles/apparel
Kimberly Clark de C.A. (USA) – Paper production and distribution facility
Maseca (Mexico) -- Corn Milling
Max (Guatemala) -- Appliance retailing
Petenatti (Brazil) -- Textiles
PriceSmart (USA) -- Member discount store and supermarket
SABMiller (South Africa) -- Beer, sodas, and other beverages
Sara Lee Knit Products (USA) -- Apparel assembly
Sears (U.S. franchise acquired by a Mexican firm) -- Retail
Unopetrol El Salvador (Honduras) -- Oil refinery; Service stations/grocery markets
Stream (USA) -- Customer service/sales call center
Sykes (USA) -- Customer service/sales call center
Telefonica de España (Spain) -- Cellular telephone service
TIGO (USA/Luxembourg) -- Cellular telephone service, cable television, landline, and internet
Texaco Caribbean (USA) -- Fuel storage and lubricant blending, and service station/grocery markets
Unifi (USA) --Yarn
Unisola-Unilever (UK) -- Consumer products
WalMart (United States) -- Supermarkets

19. CONTACT POINT AT POST FOR PUBLIC INQUIRIES

- U.S. Embassy San Salvador
- Address: Final Blvd. Santa Elena, Antiguo Cuscatlán, La Libertad, El Salvador
- Email: webmasterss@state.gov
- Website: http://sansalvador.usembassy.gov/index.html
- In addition, to reach the U.S. Foreign Commercial Service (FCS) Office directly, please contact FCS San Salvador via email at: san.salvador.office.box@mail.doc.gov

INDEX

A

abuse, viii, 51, 52, 55, 67, 69, 70, 71, 77, 79
access, ix, 9, 39, 40, 55, 57, 59, 61, 64, 68, 71, 73, 85, 87, 92, 104
accountability, 5, 38, 63, 103
accounting, 48
administrators, 94, 99, 103
age, 54, 69, 70, 76
agencies, 24, 53, 73, 74, 98
agricultural exports, 10
agricultural sector, 77
agriculture, 10, 41, 68, 76, 77, 79, 105
AIDS, 74
alien smuggling, 67
antagonism, 15
antidrug efforts, viii, 2, 23
apparel industries, 23
apparel products, 94
appointments, 5, 56
arbitration, 75, 91, 92, 93, 101
architect, 7
ARENA, vii, 2, 3, 5, 6, 8, 12, 28, 62, 76
armed conflict, 15
armed forces, 53
arrest(s), 13, 14, 30, 37, 45, 55, 56, 58
Asia, 8
assessment, 21, 23, 25, 43
assets, 25, 32, 38, 64, 94, 95, 100, 101
asylum, 27, 62
Attorney General, 12, 13, 15, 24, 37, 39, 45, 52, 55, 97, 100, 101, 103
authority(s), 5, 9, 26, 38, 52, 53, 54, 55, 56, 57, 61, 65, 66, 68, 69, 73, 83, 89, 97, 100, 105
awareness, 39, 42, 56, 69, 71, 77, 78, 102

B

bail, 55, 57
banking, 88, 99, 100
banking sector, 88
bankruptcy, 92
banks, 88, 90, 91, 99, 100
bargaining, 75
barriers, 13, 99
barriers to entry, 99
basic competencies, 47
batteries, 45
BEA, 106
beneficiaries, 41
benefits, 12, 23, 25, 39, 79, 93, 94, 95, 105
beverages, 95, 108
bias, 66
Bilateral, 19, 103
bilateral aid, 19, 20
births, 69
Bluetooth, 45
Bolivia, 29
bonds, 10, 100

bonuses, 79
border crossing, 21
brain, 26
brain drain, 26
Brazil, 48, 108
business environment, 49
businesses, 11, 12, 18, 20, 37, 38, 49, 68, 71, 79, 87, 90, 93, 95, 96, 102, 105
buyers, 100

C

Cabinet, 7, 47
cable television, 108
call centers, 89, 95, 105
campaigns, 67, 71, 77
candidates, 39, 60
capacity building, 18
capital goods, 94
capital markets, 9
Caribbean, 19, 22, 23, 29, 30, 106, 108
Caribbean countries, 23, 29
Caribbean nations, 29
CARSI, viii, 2, 17, 20, 24, 27
cash, 11, 23
Catholic Church, 82, 83
CBP, 34
cell phones, 45, 55
censorship, 55, 61
Census, 77, 81
Central American Regional Security Initiative, viii, 2, 17, 20, 24
certificate, 39, 72
certification, 6
challenges, vii, 1, 2, 3, 6, 10, 11, 12, 13, 15, 76
Chamber of Commerce, 96
chat rooms, 61
chemical, 49
child abuse, 69
child labor, 77
child pornography, 70
childcare, 102
children, viii, 2, 14, 27, 28, 43, 51, 53, 54, 66, 68, 69, 70, 71, 76, 77

Chile, ix, 46, 86, 104
circulation, 90
citizens, 25, 62, 96
civil law, 59
civil rights, 68, 84
civil service, 18, 39
civil service reform, 39
civil society, 37, 42, 60, 65, 67
civil war, 3, 8, 28, 29, 53, 102
classes, 66
cleaning, 95
climate, ix, 6, 8, 10, 12, 17, 18, 45, 46, 48, 58, 85, 86
clothing, 93
cocaine, 23
coercion, 59
coffee, 10, 22, 77, 78
Cold War, 28
collaboration, 16, 17, 42
collective bargaining, 75, 76
colleges, 47
collusion, 99
Colombia, ix, 8, 40, 86, 104, 107
commerce, x, 77, 86, 87
commercial, viii, ix, 51, 67, 69, 70, 77, 85, 86, 88, 92, 93, 96, 99
Common Market, 94, 104
communication, 15, 44
community(s), 5, 19, 20, 21, 25, 28, 41, 42, 47, 53, 63, 70, 72, 73, 74, 102
comparative advantage, 49
compensation, 59, 75
competition, 98, 99, 101
competitiveness, viii, 2, 17, 19, 23, 46
competitors, 99
complement, 20
compliance, 39, 70
complications, 59
composition, 22
compulsory education, 76
computer, 97
computer software, 97
conceptual model, 48
conciliation, 8
conditioning, 99

Index

conference, 46
conflict, vii, 1, 3, 6, 11, 15, 26, 30, 43
conflict resolution, 43
Congress, vii, 1, 2, 13, 16, 20, 28, 30, 32
connectivity, 20
consensus, 40
Constitution, 103
construction, 20, 38, 44, 60, 75, 77, 79
consulting, 17
consumers, 98
Continental, 88
controversial, 7, 9
conviction, 14, 58, 70
cooperation, viii, 16, 17, 66, 72
coordination, 37
copyright, 97, 98
corporate governance, 48
Corporate Social Responsibility, 101
corruption, viii, 2, 3, 5, 12, 13, 14, 16, 23, 37, 38, 51, 56, 57, 63, 79, 102, 103
cost, 10, 78, 98
Costa Rica, ix, 36, 86, 88, 104, 107
counsel, 57, 59, 102
counseling, 37
crimes, 11, 15, 18, 30, 37, 57, 58, 66, 70
criminal activity, 44
criminal investigations, 37
criminality, 56
criticism, 60
Cuba, 7, 8, 17, 29, 104
cultivation, 77
culture, 26
currency, 9, 46, 64, 90, 104
curriculum, 77
customer service, 36
customers, 100

denial, 69
Department of Homeland Security, 16
Department of Labor, 78
deployments, 13
Deportations, 26
deposits, 100
destruction, 97
detainees, 54, 55, 56, 57, 59
detection, 24
detention, viii, 26, 51, 52, 54, 55, 56, 57
developing nations, 31
development assistance, 49
development banks, 11
DHS, 16, 24, 26, 33
dialogues, 6, 49
digital television, 89
direct investment, 49
directors, 61, 100
disability, 66, 71
disclosure, 65
discrimination, viii, ix, 51, 53, 66, 68, 71, 72, 73, 74, 75, 76, 81, 82, 83, 99
distortions, 98
distribution, 95, 97, 98, 101, 104, 105, 107, 108
doctors, 53, 59, 71
domestic violence, viii, 51, 67
Dominican Republic, ix, 10, 20, 22, 33, 86, 103
donations, 3, 82
donors, 10, 17, 41, 42
draft, 39, 45
drug smuggling, 24
drug trafficking, 8, 12, 24, 52
drugs, 23, 45, 54
due process, 103
duty-free access, 23

D

damages, 55, 59
database, 47
deaths, 3
defendants, 59
Delta, 46
democracy, 3

E

earthquakes, 3, 26
economic assistance, 31
economic cooperation, viii, 2
economic growth, vii, 1, 3, 5, 9, 17, 32, 38, 40

Index

economic growth rate, vii, 1
economic policy, 10
economic reform(s), 3
economic well-being, 37
Ecuador, 29, 104
editors, 61
education, 8, 11, 19, 20, 27, 42, 47, 67, 69, 71, 73, 77, 83, 102
educational opportunities, 42, 72, 77
election, vii, 2, 3, 6, 28, 40, 102
electricity, 21, 89, 98, 107, 108
electromagnetic, 98
electronic surveillance, 44
elementary school, 77
e-mail, 61
embassy, ix, 81, 84
emergency, 60
emigration, viii, 2, 3, 26, 62
employees, 39, 64, 68, 75, 76, 78, 87, 89, 90, 93, 95, 103, 105
employers, 68, 74, 75, 76, 77, 78, 79, 89, 105
employment, 18, 41, 47, 68, 71, 72, 73, 74, 76, 87
energy, 8, 10, 11, 46, 89, 91, 99, 101
energy supply, 91
enforcement, ix, 24, 52, 56, 67, 71, 96, 97, 103
environment, ix, 11, 19, 45, 85, 86, 87, 98
environmental awareness, 84
equipment, 12, 20, 22, 23, 38, 39, 44, 78, 89, 93, 94, 95, 97
equity, 89
ethics, 103
ethnic minority, 63
Europe, 8
European Parliament, 104
European Union (EU), ix, 86, 104
evidence, 30, 36, 45, 56, 57, 58, 64
exchange rate, 9, 46
exclusion, 73
executive branch, 5, 60, 67
Executive Order, 25, 33
exercise, 54, 72
exploitation, viii, 51, 67, 69, 70, 72, 77, 79

exports, 10, 22, 23, 48, 49, 94
exposure, 46
external shocks, 9
extraction, 87, 91
extradition, 16, 45

F

families, 15, 21, 26, 77
family planning, 68
Farabundo Marti National Liberation Front, vii, viii, 1, 3, 51, 101
farmers, 20
farms, 44
FBI, 24, 27
FDI, ix, 9, 10, 18, 48, 85, 86, 88, 106, 107
FDI inflow, 88, 106
FDIC, 100
fear, 58, 61, 66, 68, 69, 74
Federal Bureau of Investigation (FBI), 24
female prisoners, 54
fertilizers, 107
fetus, 59
financial, 10, 11, 17, 20, 22, 25, 29, 71, 95, 98, 99, 100, 101
financial crimes, 22
financial crisis, 10, 11, 25
financial institutions, 100
financial intermediaries, 99
financial resources, 71
financial stability, 98
financial support, 29
fiscal deficit, 10
fishing, 77, 96, 108
FMLN, vii, viii, 1, 2, 3, 4, 6, 7, 8, 13, 16, 22, 28, 29, 32, 51, 62, 76, 101, 102
food, 79, 95, 101
food production, 101
force, ix, 13, 18, 24, 38, 52, 86, 92, 99, 103, 104
foreign aid, 16, 17
foreign banks, 100
foreign companies, 93
foreign direct investment, 9, 86

foreign investment, vii, ix, 1, 10, 48, 85, 86, 87, 89
foreign policy, 17
formal education, 42
formal sector, 77, 79
foundations, 82, 84, 102
France, 108
franchise, 108
fraud, 16
free trade, ix, 18, 86, 90, 93, 94, 103, 104, 105
freedom, viii, ix, 18, 32, 51, 59, 60, 61, 62, 75, 76, 81, 82, 83, 84
funding, viii, 2, 12, 15, 19, 25, 27, 43, 56, 58, 72
funds, 19, 20, 21, 28, 41, 79, 90, 100, 105

G

gangs, vii, 2, 5, 8, 11, 14, 15, 24, 26, 30, 43, 54, 61, 77
GAO, 20, 32
garbage, 77
gender identity, 66
general education, 105
Geneva Convention, 97
Germany, 88
GHP, 19
GOES, 36, 37, 38, 39, 40, 41, 42, 43, 44, 45, 46, 47, 48, 49
goods and services, 93, 95, 98
governance, 12, 16, 23
government spending, 9
governments, viii, 2, 3, 12, 17, 18, 22, 87
grants, 25, 56, 68, 82, 87, 90
grassroots, 49
Gross Domestic Product (GDP), 10, 23, 26, 47, 48, 49, 106, 107
growth, 8, 9, 10, 17, 22, 37, 46, 89
growth rate, 9, 10, 22
Guatemala, ix, 11, 19, 22, 27, 28, 86, 88, 104, 107, 108
guerrilla commander, vii, 2, 7
guilt, 55, 58
guilty, 16

H

harassment, 53, 67, 68, 73
harvesting, 77
health, 5, 19, 54, 59, 67, 71, 73, 75, 76, 78, 79, 102
health care, 71, 73
hemisphere, 24
heroin, 23
high school, 47, 69, 73
high school degree, 73
highways, 11
hiring, 71, 74
Hispanic population, 25
history, 3, 8, 27, 28
HIV, ix, 52, 74, 102
HIV/AIDS, ix, 52, 74, 102
homicide, vii, 2, 11, 14, 52, 54, 56, 78
homicide rates, vii, 2, 14
Honduras, ix, 11, 13, 19, 21, 22, 27, 28, 30, 86, 104, 107, 108
honesty, 7
host, 90, 105
hotel(s), 24, 95, 107
housing, 102
hub, 88
human, viii, ix, 3, 5, 12, 13, 15, 17, 20, 23, 28, 51, 52, 53, 55, 56, 58, 59, 65, 72, 73, 85, 87
human capital, ix, 23, 85, 87
human development, 20
Human Development Index, 11
human right(s), viii, 3, 5, 12, 13, 15, 28, 51, 52, 55, 56, 58, 59, 65, 72, 73
human rights problems, viii, 51
humanitarian organizations, 62
hurricanes, 3

I

ICE, 16, 24, 27, 31
identification, 53, 73
identity, 63, 72, 73
image, 48

IMF, 10, 29
immigrants, 26, 33
immigration, 15, 27, 33
Immigration and Customs Enforcement (ICE), 15
imports, 22, 93, 95
imprisonment, 66, 67, 70
improvements, 21, 46
inadmissible, 57
incidence, 67
income, 9, 17, 61, 78, 94, 95, 99
income tax, 94, 95
indigenous peoples, 72
individuals, 12, 25, 28, 53, 58, 60, 68, 72, 74, 101, 102
industry(s), 23, 69, 75, 77, 79, 88, 89, 101, 104
inefficiency, 14, 57
inequality, 3, 10, 11
inflation, 9
informal sector, 75, 76, 77, 79
information technology, 95
infrastructure, ix, 8, 10, 12, 17, 21, 46, 47, 85, 87
initiation, 27
injuries, 53, 67
inmates, 14, 44, 54, 55
innocence, 58
insecurity, 17, 19, 36, 40
inspections, 75, 79
inspectors, 77, 79
institutions, 17, 20, 36, 37, 42, 49, 99, 100, 102
insurgency, vii, 1, 3
integrity, 53
intellectual property, 87, 97, 103
intellectual property rights, 97
intelligence, 12, 24, 52
Inter-American Development Bank, 10, 48
interest rates, 9, 99
interference, 66, 72
internally displaced, 62
International Monetary Fund, 10, 29, 107
International Narcotics Control, 30
international standards, 22

international trade, 93
intimidation, 58, 61
investment(s), vii, ix, 1, 8, 10, 17, 18, 20, 21, 23, 45, 46, 48, 85, 86, 87, 90, 92, 93, 95, 96, 98, 99, 101, 102, 103, 104
investors, 18, 21, 22, 48, 87, 89, 90, 92, 93, 98, 99, 102, 103, 105
IPR, 97
Israel, 108
issues, vii, viii, 2, 16, 18, 22, 27, 39, 40, 84, 98
Italy, 88

J

Jews, 82
job skills, 45
job training, 11, 18
journalists, 61
judiciary, viii, 14, 51, 57, 63
juries, 58
jurisdiction, 29, 76, 92, 93

L

labor force, 10, 38, 47, 96, 105
labor laws, ix, 52, 77, 105
labor market, 21, 26, 47
lack of confidence, 12, 63
land acquisition, 95
languages, 72
laptop, 45
Latin America, i, ii, iii, viii, 2, 8, 16, 19, 28, 29, 30, 33, 106
law enforcement, 12, 24, 25, 27
laws, ix, x, 52, 66, 68, 70, 72, 75, 76, 77, 79, 81, 82, 86, 87, 97, 98, 102, 105
laws and regulations, 98
lawyers, 98
lead, vii, 2, 4, 5, 8, 14, 18
leadership, 13, 36, 41, 43, 58
Leahy, 31
learning, 42
legal issues, 97

legality, 56
legislation, viii, x, 2, 5, 9, 18, 22, 24, 46, 48, 86, 87, 99
lending, 100, 101
LGBT, ix, 52, 53, 66, 73, 74
light, 64, 76
loans, 10, 11, 72, 88, 99
logistics, 88
lubricants, 94

M

machinery, 22, 60, 77, 93, 94
majority, viii, 2, 8, 9, 75, 93
man, 73
management, 24, 36, 44, 105
manipulation, 92
manpower, 23
marijuana, 23
market position, 99
marketplace, 98
marriage, 69
married women, 68
Maryland, 46
materials, 39, 44, 70
matrix, 89
Mauricio Funes, vii, viii, 1, 3, 4, 14, 16, 28, 51, 102
media, 6, 25, 40, 52, 55, 60, 61, 64, 73, 89
mediation, 55, 56, 67, 75
medical, 54, 74, 89, 95
medical care, 54
membership, 30, 74, 83
mental health, 71
mentoring, 39
messengers, 79
metallurgy, 105
metropolitan areas, 95
Mexico, ix, 22, 26, 27, 33, 86, 88, 104, 107, 108
Miami, 31
migrants, 25, 26, 28, 33
migration, viii, 2, 26, 27
military, 5, 7, 12, 13, 15, 24, 28, 31, 52, 53, 56

minimum wage, 78, 79
Ministry of Education, 42, 77, 83
minorities, 53, 63, 73
minors, 27, 28, 30, 70, 77
mission, 84
modernization, 18, 46
modules, 48
mollusks, 77
money laundering, 11, 22, 24
monopoly, 101
Multilateral, 105
multinational companies, 22
multinational firms, 92
murder, 15, 53
Muslims, 82

N

narcotics, 23, 61
national income, 90
national security, 45, 56
national strategy, 25, 41, 43
Nationalist Republican Alliance, vii, 2, 3
nationality, 82, 96
natural disaster(s), 3, 26
natural resources, 72
negotiating, ix, 86, 104
negotiation, 75
Netherlands, 108
NGOs, 28, 53, 55, 63, 65, 67, 73, 83
Nicaragua, ix, 23, 29, 86, 104, 107
nursing, 69

O

Obama, 16, 17, 20, 24, 25, 27, 28
Obama Administration, 16, 17, 20, 24, 25, 27, 28
occupational health, 78
OECD, 103
offenders, 44, 54, 55, 67, 82
Office of the Inspector General, 52

officials, ix, 7, 12, 13, 14, 16, 17, 20, 22, 23, 24, 25, 27, 28, 36, 42, 52, 53, 63, 64, 65, 81, 82, 84, 103
oil, 22, 29, 89, 101
operations, 21, 30, 37, 48, 87, 89, 93, 95, 99, 100
opportunities, 21, 26, 27, 41, 72
Organization of American States, 14, 103
organize, 40, 75, 105
outreach, 25, 40, 105
outsourcing, 95, 105
overlay, 46
overpopulation, 54
Overseas Private Investment Corporation, 104
oversight, 38
overtime, 78, 79
ownership, 32, 88, 89

P

Pacific, 23, 24, 33, 91
Panama, ix, 3, 86, 88, 104, 107, 108
parents, 27, 42, 69, 71
participants, 41, 44, 47, 99
Partnership for Growth, v, viii, ix, 2, 8, 10, 16, 17, 23, 32, 33, 35, 85, 87
patents, 90, 97
peace, 3, 102
peace accord, 3, 102
penalties, 30, 63, 67, 70, 74, 75, 78, 102
permit, 66, 77, 89, 96
perpetrators, 15, 52, 58, 73
persons with disabilities, ix, 52, 55, 66, 71, 72
Peru, ix, 86, 104
PFG, viii, ix, 2, 7, 10, 16, 17, 18, 23, 32, 37, 40, 85, 87
pharmaceuticals, 49, 97
Philippines, 32
physical abuse, 53, 67
physical health, 79
piracy, 97
plants, 93, 96, 108
plastics, 49

platform, 7
pneumonia, 53
polarization, 6
police, ix, 5, 7, 12, 13, 14, 15, 22, 24, 25, 27, 30, 37, 38, 41, 52, 53, 54, 56, 58, 67, 73, 74
policy, 5, 32, 33, 71
political party(s), 3, 58, 62, 63, 76
pollution, 58
population, vii, 1, 20, 39, 43, 54, 57, 67, 75, 79, 81
portfolio, 88, 100
portfolio investment, 100
poverty, 9, 10, 11, 20, 72, 78
predatory pricing, 99
preferential treatment, 96, 101
pregnancy, 59, 68
preparation, 18, 48
presidency, vii, 1, 102
president, vii, viii, 2, 3, 5, 6, 7, 8, 9, 10, 11, 12, 13, 14, 15, 16, 17, 23, 24, 25, 27, 31, 33, 39, 40, 45, 51, 56, 60, 65, 66, 67, 82, 103
President Obama, 16, 23
presidential campaign, 7
presumption of innocence, 58
pretrial detention, viii, 51, 54, 57
prevention, 5, 13, 17, 19, 25, 27, 38, 40, 41, 42, 43
principles, vii, 2, 15, 32, 83
prison conditions, viii, 51
prisoners, 14, 54, 55, 59
prisons, 12, 14, 43, 44, 54, 55
private investment, 21
private ownership, 91
private schools, 83
private sector, vii, 2, 3, 5, 6, 8, 11, 17, 18, 19, 40, 42, 43, 45, 49, 88, 93, 101, 105
privatization, 100
procurement, 22, 44, 48, 104
producers, 11, 21, 23, 94
professionals, 26, 36
program administration, 32
programming, 60
project, 18, 20, 21, 46, 49, 77, 89, 104

Index

proliferation, 19
propane, 98
protection, 58, 59, 62, 64, 97, 103
puberty, 69
public awareness, 67
public officials, 52, 53, 68, 73, 103
public opinion, 41
public resources, 47, 48
public schools, 40
public sector, 74, 94
public service, 20, 21
public-private partnerships, 10, 42
publishing, 65
PUMA, 108
punishment, 53

Q

query, 107
questioning, 54, 57

R

race, 66, 82
radio, 61, 89
rape, 66, 67, 69, 70
raw materials, 93
reading, 90
real estate, 79, 89, 94, 96
reception, 89
recession, 10, 11
recognition, 82
recommendations, 38, 66
reconstruction, 79
recovery, 10
reform(s), x, 8, 10, 13, 21, 22, 26, 30, 32, 43, 45, 48, 72, 86, 87, 89, 90, 91, 92, 93, 97, 98
refugee status, 62
refugees, 62
regional integration, 20
Registry, 92, 97, 100
regulations, ix, 44, 85, 86, 90, 93, 94, 96, 97, 102

rehabilitation, 20, 40, 41, 46
reimburse, 25
relief, 3, 33
religion, 82
religious beliefs, 82
remittances, 9, 26, 90
renewable energy, 46, 89
repair, 88, 89, 95
repatriate, 90
repression, 72
reputation, 7, 48
requirements, 71, 74, 76, 83, 92, 100, 104
resolution, 55, 86, 92
resources, 14, 42, 44, 58, 66, 69, 70, 71, 74, 77, 87
response, 21, 33, 56, 59, 83
restrictions, viii, 40, 51, 60, 61, 74, 75, 89, 90, 96
retail, 78, 98, 108
retaliation, 61
revenue, 10, 72
rights, viii, 3, 5, 12, 13, 15, 16, 29, 48, 52, 55, 56, 58, 59, 60, 61, 62, 65, 66, 68, 71, 72, 73, 74, 75, 76, 79, 92, 97, 101, 103
risk(s), 18, 25, 41, 42, 43, 44, 59, 68, 78, 79
root, 27
rule of law, 8, 15, 58
rules, 56, 93, 94, 104
rules of origin, 104
runoff, vii, 2, 6
rural areas, 78

S

safety, 78, 79
Salvador Sánchez Cerén, vii, 1, 2, 3, 5, 6, 7, 29, 102
San Salvador, 6, 7, 30, 33, 40, 41, 49, 94, 109
sanctions, 24, 25, 56, 60, 63, 64, 65
savings, 88, 100
scaling, 48
school, 5, 18, 19, 25, 42, 43, 69, 71, 72, 73, 77, 83
school activities, 42

school enrollment, 69
schooling, 21
science, 47
security(s), vii, viii, 1, 2, 4, 5, 7, 8, 10, 12, 13, 15, 16, 18, 23, 24, 27, 31, 38, 40, 44, 51, 52, 53, 56, 58, 75, 84, 100
security assistance, viii, 2
security forces, viii, 12, 51
security guard, 12, 75
seed, 22, 41, 104
seizure, 97
seminars, 47
sensitivity, 71
sentencing, 57, 58
September 11, 31, 62, 73
service industries, 77
service provider, 89
services, 20, 37, 42, 49, 70, 71, 75, 78, 89, 90, 93, 94, 95, 98, 100
sex, 70
sexual abuse, 55, 67, 68, 69, 71
sexual harassment, 67, 68, 79
sexual orientation, 66, 73
sexual violence, 37
shareholders, 90, 100
shelter, 69, 70
signals, 45, 97
small businesses, 18, 77
Smuggling, 54
social benefits, 15
social justice, 8
social programs, 5, 6, 7, 11
social responsibility, 101
social security, 79
social status, 66
society, viii, 2, 6, 13, 16, 40, 44, 64, 65
software, 89
South Africa, 108
Spain, 5, 16, 29, 88, 107, 108
speech, viii, 51, 60
spending, 10, 11, 26
Spring, 30
stability, 9
stakeholders, 48

state(s), 9, 29, 30, 32, 57, 61, 70, 71, 72, 76, 78, 82, 86, 87, 88, 90, 100, 101, 109
state enterprises, 100
state-owned banks, 88
state-owned enterprises, 9, 101
statistics, 41, 69
statutes, 70, 87
stock, 99, 106
storage, 108
structure, 38
subsidy, 98
sugarcane, 77
suicide, 54
Supreme Court, 3, 5, 6, 9, 13, 15, 29, 31, 36, 45, 56, 57, 58, 63, 64, 67, 92, 97, 101
surveillance, 38
survival, 77
survivors, 15

T

Taiwan, ix, 3, 86, 104
talent, 105
Tanzania, 32
target, 10, 41, 88
tariff, 23, 98
Task Force, 24, 37, 38
tax credits, 90, 93
tax evasion, 48
taxation, 95
taxes, 8, 12, 90, 93, 94, 95
teacher training, 21
teachers, 42, 47, 71, 79
teams, 37
technical assistance, 20, 21, 38, 39, 47, 90
techniques, 38
technology, 47, 89, 93, 95, 105
telecommunications, 89, 98
telephone, 67, 70, 108
television advertisements, 60
temperature, 54
territory, 90
test data, 97
testing, 68
textiles, 22, 49, 105

Index

theatre, 42
threats, 20, 52, 61, 76, 79
tobacco, 95
torture, 12, 53
total energy, 89
tourism, 89, 95
trade, ix, 8, 10, 18, 22, 44, 86, 90, 92, 101, 104
trade agreement, ix, 22, 86, 92, 104
trademarks, 90, 97
trafficking, ix, 7, 11, 51, 61, 67, 70
trafficking in persons, ix, 51, 67
training, 12, 14, 18, 20, 23, 24, 36, 38, 39, 41, 43, 44, 47, 56, 58, 71, 78, 79, 102
transactions, 25, 90, 100
transparency, vii, 2, 5, 8, 37, 38, 39, 48, 63, 91
transplant, 105
transport, 44, 98
transportation, 38, 44, 71, 88, 95, 101, 102
Treasury, 25, 33, 38
treaties, 39
treatment, viii, 37, 51, 53, 68, 72, 87, 93, 100, 104
trial, 5, 29, 37, 52, 57, 58
turnout, 6

U

U.S. assistance, 17, 24
U.S.-Salvadoran relations, vii, 1, 2, 16
UK, 102, 108
UNDP, 73
UNHCR, 33, 62
union representatives, 75
unions, 74, 75, 76, 79, 99, 105
United, vii, ix, 1, 2, 3, 7, 8, 10, 15, 16, 17, 20, 22, 23, 24, 25, 26, 27, 28, 31, 32, 33, 34, 45, 47, 85, 86, 87, 88, 90, 91, 96, 103, 104, 106, 107, 108
United Nations (UN), 31, 57, 58, 62, 72, 73, 103, 106
United States, vii, ix, 1, 2, 3, 7, 8, 10, 15, 16, 17, 20, 22, 23, 24, 25, 26, 27, 32, 33, 34, 45, 47, 85, 86, 87, 88, 90, 91, 96, 103, 104, 107, 108
updating, 38
urban, 41, 78
urban areas, 78
urban youth, 41
USA, 107, 108

V

Valencia, 29
value added tax, 93
vehicles, 37, 95
Venezuela, viii, 2, 6, 7, 8, 17, 29, 101, 107
ventilation, 54
venue, 92
vessels, 95
Vice President, 5, 6, 7, 27
victims, 3, 5, 15, 37, 58, 66, 67, 68, 69, 70
violence, ix, 3, 8, 12, 14, 17, 19, 25, 27, 37, 40, 41, 43, 52, 53, 58, 67, 68, 69, 73, 78, 102
violent crime, vii, ix, 2, 16, 58, 85, 86
violent criminals, 54
vocational training, 41, 43
volatility, 98
vote, 6, 9
voters, viii, 6, 28, 51, 62
voting, 6, 28

W

wages, 95
war, 3, 7, 15, 102
war years, 7
Washington, 26, 28, 29, 30
water, 21, 54, 98
watershed, 28
weakness, 13
wealth, 28
weapons, 14, 45, 54, 77
web, 39, 48
web service, 48
websites, 40

White House, 33, 34
wholesale, 98
witnesses, 58, 63
worker rights, 65
workers, 47, 60, 68, 74, 75, 76, 77, 78, 79
workforce, 20
workplace, 68, 72, 78, 79, 102
World Bank, 10, 29, 42, 69, 91

World Trade Organization (WTO), 90, 93, 94, 104

young people, 43